# Paddling Partners

## Fifty Years of Northern Canoe Travel

# Paddling Partners

## Fifty Years of Northern Canoe Travel

Bruce W. Hodgins & Carol Hodgins

NATURAL HERITAGE BOOKS
A MEMBER OF THE DUNDURN GROUP
TORONTO

Published by Natural Heritage Books
A Member of The Dundurn Group
3 Church Street, Suite 500
Toronto, Ontario, M5E 1M2, Canada
www.dundurn.com

**Library and Archives Canada Cataloguing in Publication**
Hodgins, Bruce W., 1931-
    Paddling partners : fifty years of northern canoe travel / Bruce W. Hodgins, Carol Hodgins.

Includes index.
ISBN 978-1-55002-761-7

    1. Hodgins, Bruce W., 1931- --Travel.  2. Hodgins, Carol--Travel.  3. Canoes and canoeing--Canada.  4. Canoeists--Canada--Biography.  5. Canoes and canoeing.  I. Hodgins, Carol  II. Title.

GV782.42.H64A3 2008        797.122'092271        C2007-904657-6

1 2 3 4 5 1 1 1 0 0 9 0 8 0 7

All visuals supplied by the authors. Photo on page 147, on the Atlawapiskat River, courtesy of Shelagh Grant.
Cover and text design by Erin Mallory
Edited by Jane Gibson
Printed and bound in Canada by Transcontinental

Care has been taken to trace the ownership of copyright material used in this book. The author and the publisher welcome any information enabling them to rectify any references or credits in subsequent editions.

*J. Kirk Howard, President*

We acknowledge the support of the **Canada Council for the Arts** and the **Ontario Arts Council** for our publishing program. We also acknowledge the financial support of the **Government of Canada** through the **Book Publishing Industry Development Program** and **The Association for the Export of Canadian Books** and the **Government of Ontario** through the **Ontario Book Publishers Tax Credit Program** and the **Ontario Media Development Corporation.**

To our five grandchildren, Holly and Kayla Nesbitt, Bronwyn, Alexander and Frieda Hodgins—canoe trippers all!

# Contents

PART THREE: FROM NORTHERN ONTARIO TO THE FAR NORTH, 1980–1989

PART FOUR: NEAR AND FAR: NORTH AND SOUTH, 1990–1999

PART FIVE: THE NEW MILLENNIUM AND NEW ADVENTURES,
          2000–2007

# Acknowledgements

We, Carol and Bruce Hodgins, have been paddling partners since 1957. We have paddled together each of these years and led canoe trips during a great majority of those years. Most of our canoe trips have been of two weeks duration, some of three weeks and several of only a week. In some years we have taken two trips, occasionally three, and for a very few years it was only spring and summer day paddles. Most of the time the trips have been in the Canadian North, broadly defined to include both the provincial and territorial North.

We have canoed in all ten provinces (Newfoundland in 2007) and all three territories and out onto Canada's three oceans. We have also canoed—and here the word includes kayaking—in Mexico's Baja California, in the Florida Everglades, and have been on several day trips in various parts of Australia.

In this volume we share many of our experiences and adventures and those of our fellow companions, many of whom have become our close lifelong friends. Nearly all of our canoe trips have been with either Camp Wanapitei or Wanapitei Canoe Northern Expeditions Inc. (C.A.N.O.E.) and since 1973, mostly with adults.

Overall about 300 different individuals have canoed-tripped with us, and in our tripping accounts we include many of the names of the participants who have gone with us on five or more trips. Shelagh Grant has participated in eleven trips, her husband Jon on eight. Bill Cormode has been with us on ten trips (including a northern Georgian Bay excursion in August 2007) and his partner Cathryn Rees on eight. (E.J) Ted Moores went with Bruce on six trips, while cousin Daryl Hodgins, John Scott and Diana Paterson were also on six. Dr. Tom Morley, Dr. Bill Paterson, Dr. Ken Shonk and Carol's niece Meredith and husband

Elliot Rodger have gone on five. The following people were on three or four trips with us: Doreen and Myk Bartlett, Dr. Barry Diceman, Al Gamble (deceased), Dave Goslin, Barbara Hodgins, Gwyneth Hoyle, Richard Mansfield, Robin Maughan, Lynda (deceased June 2007) and Don Mason, Lynn McDonald, Alan Norris, Louise Rohanczy, Larry and Sharon Pearson and Dr Michael Watts. Many of these friends have become a vital part of our lives; we thank them all for their support.

The Peterborough-based spring Canoe Group came together in the late sixties, changed profoundly in the late seventies, flourished in the eighties and nineties, and now thrives in 2007. The Group features day trips on the middle range, whitewater rivers in east-central Ontario. The following individuals have paddled with our Group for over fifteen years: Bill Cormode and Cathryn Rees, John and Nicola Jennings, Dale and Bernice Standen, Barry Diceman, Dave Goslin, Shelagh and Jon Grant, Heather Dunlop, and especially in the broad middle years our sons Shawn and Geoff Hodgins, and cousins Glenn and Eric, and Gwyneth Hoyle. Hilary Heath, Bev Haun, John Moss, Jean Manore and Dale Miner, and Larry and Sharon Pearson have paddled with us for almost as many years. Two other close friends, Jamie Benidickson and Alistair Thomas, in the early years paddled with us. Many of those listed above have authored, co-authored, edited or co-edited with Bruce, articles or books on the role or history of the canoe, canoe travel, or the North. More than a few of the above have been actively involved with Wanapitei. Many have been important, some very important, with regard to the founding and enhancement of the Canadian Canoe Museum. Many have participated in the annual winter Canoeing and Wilderness Symposium held in Toronto and organized by George Luste. For most of these people their friendship, affection and support have made our continuing canoe paddling partnership possible and enjoyable as we have now moved into our mid-seventies.

Thanks to Myrna Greer for all her help in putting the initial part of this project onto the computer. Also thanks to Nicola Jennings for her careful reading of the manuscript.

Finally, this volume would never have come about without the suggestions, encouragement and editing by Barry Penhale and Jane Gibson at Natural Heritage Books: A Member of the Dundurn Group.

# Introduction

We became paddling partners and began co-leading canoe trips in August 1957, along with other camp staff and a rather large co-ed youth group. This was for Camp Wanapitei on Lake Temagami in northeastern Ontario.[1] Bruce was program director. His parents, Stanley and Laura Belle Hodgins, the camp co-directors, had purchased Wanapitei from Ed Archibald in 1956. Previously, Bruce had experienced his first canoe trip, as a camper, for three days in 1943 in Haliburton out of Camp Kilcoo. From 1944 to 1955 he was a camper, a counsellor, a trip leader, then program director, for the Kitchener-Waterloo YMCA Camp Wabanaki, on northern Beausoliel Island near Honey Harbour. During those years, Bruce tripped the Muskosh, Gibson, Severn rivers and the Six Mile Lake area inland from Georgian Bay.

Carol grew up in Charlottetown, Prince Edward Island. She had some camping, sailing and boating experience and had done lots of swimming but no canoe tripping. She did, however, love the out-of-doors. In her early years virtually no one on Prince Edward Island even owned a canoe, but relatives in Nova Scotia did. Her cousin Ann (Creighton) Buik recently recollected how annoyed her mother had been with her at their cottage near Lunenburg, when as young teenagers she and a friend spent three hours in the rain, paddling their canoe around Herman's Island. No one had any idea where they were.

We met in the autumn of 1956 while Bruce was teaching at Prince of Wales College and Carol was a physiotherapist at the Rehab Centre in Charlottetown, treating a broad variety of patients, but mainly those recovering from polio. They were both mentoring local HI-Y Clubs. Bruce, as an historian and a "political animal" and very interested in foreign affairs, was frequently invited to speak at dinners across the Island. It was the autumn of 1956, the time of the Suez and Hungarian crises. Carol usually accompanied him on the "rubber chicken circuit," and they spent much time talking about their interests.

Carol's first trip to Wanapitei was in the summer of 1957, and her first canoe trip was on the Lady Evelyn River with its many challenging portages. For the first three days it seemed like misery. Her pack seemed to weigh a ton, she fell and tears rolled down her cheeks, and she was so sore her bones ached, particularly at night when there was no thermarest to act as a cushion. However, there was a gradual gain in strength and loss of pain and an awareness of the beauty of the area and of the fun experienced with the wonderful group of teenagers with whom we were canoeing. She never looked back. Having grown up by the sea on the largely pastoral Island, she found the rugged Northern Ontario landscape overwhelming but pleasurable. To be able to fish in the same water as one brushed one's teeth and drink the water (then), and not always have to tie up a boat at a lunch spot took some time to adjust her thinking.

The biggest disappointment upon returning to the Island was not to be able to have others understand what a canoe trip in Northern Ontario was like. At that time she had no idea what lay ahead. The memory has somewhat faded now, but during the first full summer in "the north," her head was covered in almost egg-size bumps from blackflies who discovered some tender juices never before exposed to the "likes of them."

The friendship and love between us deepened. We were married in July of 1958 and Carol worked for two years, 1958–60, in the Physical Therapy Department, at Duke University Medical Centre, Durham, North Carolina, while Bruce was working on his PhD in History at Duke.

Since then we have been paddling partners every year. For several years during the sixties, however, when sons Shawn and Geoff were too young to be integrated into the camp, Carol stayed back on site rather than go on the longer trips. Since 1979, Shawn has been leading canoe trips, the majority in the Far North. Today, he and his wife Liz McCarney own Wanapitei C.A.N.O.E. Geoff began leading canoe trips in 1981 with Pat Bowles who later became his wife. Holly Nesbitt, our first grandchild to do so, co-led youth trips for Wanapitei in the summer of 2007. She had spent many years as a tripping camper, including the 2006 two-month expedition crossing the Rockies' divide (in the Yukon) to the Bonnet Plume River. Our other four grandchildren, Kayla Nesbitt, Bronwyn, Alexander and Frieda Hodgins have also been participating as campers on Wanapitei canoe trips — a true family affair.

Since 1965 we have lived, off summer, in Peterborough where Bruce was a professor of History and Canadian Studies at Trent University until his retirement in 1996 and Carol worked part time as a physiotherapist at the Peterborough Clinic. At Wanapitei, Carol ran the  Trip Stores (Sangego) for the Camp from 1967 until 1987. She has written two canoe-tripping cookbooks.[2] Bruce was the program director for Wanapitei from 1956 to 1970 and summer camp director from 1971 until 1993 and continues to be Wanapitei's president.

We co-led Wanapitei canoe trips for many decades, but since 1973 these have been mainly adult trips. Our early trips in the North, which we loved, only made us and many of our canoeing partners want to see more.

Over the years we have always felt very comfortable paddling together. One time when Bruce shouted, "Watch for the rock," which I (Carol) had already seen but thought he must have meant a different one. I did a hard draw that landed us on top of a third rock. By this time I was "reading the water" quite well, so a quick two-person conference was held and we continued on as  very good canoeing partners and friends. We did discover, however, that some couples had to be in separate canoes on trips. Like most others we had our ups and downs, but the "ups" won out, and our love of canoeing and the North and its people became very important to us.

In 2003, we tripped on the lower Bloodvein River with some of our long-time, experienced canoeing friends from past northern trips. Some of them organized the trip and the leadership was shared. Bruce still teaches canoeing at Wanapitei as an Ontario Recreational Canoeing and Kayaking Association (ORCKA) instructor and examiner.

We still canoe, but with less vigour. Each spring we begin with our long-time Canoe Group soon after the ice goes out and paddle on rivers in central Ontario. In mid-July 2007 we participated in a kayak trip off Newfoundland, planned in conjunction with C.A.N.O.E. and led by our son Shawn. In mid-August we went on a short Near North canoe trip out from the west end of Collins Inlet and Philip Edward Island on north Georgian Bay with four long-time canoeing friends, Nicola and John Jennings, Bill Cormode and Cathryn Rees.

This volume recounts the story of our shared canoe travel from 1957 to the present. Until recently, on most trips we were the co-leaders, with the majority of the outings having been in the North, broadly defined. Initially, this primarily meant northeastern Ontario centred in Temagami and northwestern Quebec, in the Kipawa, Dumoine, Noire and Bazin watersheds. There would, however, be four "Bay Trips" to James or Hudson Bay, (the 1961 trip without Carol), two trips in northern Saskatchewan, one in northern Manitoba, three in the Yukon, four in the present-day Northwest Territories and five in the Nunavut Territory. We would lead a trip and briefly paddle out onto Canada's three oceans, the Atlantic, Pacific and Arctic.

Altogether we have paddled in all ten provinces (Newfoundland in July 2007) and all three territories. Our first trip north of 60 was in 1976 on the South Nahanni, then followed by the Coppermine River in 1979. In 1993, we paddled on the first of our three trips on the Soper River on Baffin Island, now part of Nunavut. During three winters, 1997–99, we took kayak trips in Baja California Sur, Mexico, and in the summer of 2000 we kayaked along the coastline among some of the islands in the Queen Charlottes (Haida Gwaii) in northern British Columbia. In the winter of 1997 we, along with another leader, Jeff Edwards, took a group to canoe in the Everglades of Florida. In 1998, we canoed on three of the Heritage Rivers in the Maritimes. On our various trips to Australia we went on day paddles in Victoria, New South Wales and Queensland.

What follows is a description of our routes and our fascinating adventures, usually with at least one day taken directly from the log of the trips. Also included are pictures from many of the trips and several sketch maps that identify most of the routes.

Why have we been, for these fifty years such committed canoe trippers? We did it because we loved it. We revel in the northern wilderness, the word now verbally refigured to include and to have included a "light" human presence, largely Aboriginal. In contrast to great canoeist Herb Pohl[3] who died on a solo canoe trip in July 2006 just off the shore of Lake Superior, we paddling partners have almost always paddled in the same boat with a collectivity of canoes and people of both gender. So the "trip" includes the route, the boats, the portages, the trippers, the fellowship, the deepening friendships, the experiences and the lasting memories. The canoes as vessels blend with the participants as friends and the environment as sanctuary.

# List of Maps

# PART ONE:

# THE TRIPPING TOGETHER BEGINS, 1957–1969

# 1

## THE TEMAGAMI COUNTRY AND BEYOND, 1957–1960

The village of Temagami is about eighty-five kilometres north of North Bay, Ontario. It is there because that is where the railway (the Temiskaming and Northern Ontario Railway, now known as the Ontario Northland [ONR]) went through. Since 1926 it has also been on what is now Highway 11. The village, established in 1905, is at the northeast end of the complex octopus-like Lake Temagami, the outlet of which flows south through the Temagami and French rivers to Lake Nipissing and the French River to Georgian Bay.

Just north of Lake Temagami is the Lady Evelyn/Montreal watershed flowing to Lake Temiskaming and the Ottawa River. North of that watershed is the James Bay watershed. The Temagami-Lady Evelyn country is all headwaters country. Camp Wanapitei, since 1931 has been situated in the extreme north-central part of the Lake where the Red Squirrel River enters Ferguson Bay.

In 1888, Robert Bell of the Geological Survey inappropriately named the Lady Evelyn River (and Lake) for an obscure young beauty of Scottish aristocracy, Evelyn Catherine Campbell, eighth child of the Duke of Argyle. She had earlier visited her brother the Governor General, the Marquis of Lorne, at Rideau Hall and there had met Robert Bell. Yet locally the river was still called by the Anishnabai name Majamaygas, "the Trout Streams," which was approached by Namabinnagasheshingue, Sucker Gut Lake, when in 1903 James Edward Jones wrote about it so glowingly in *Camping and Canoeing*. In 1918 Jones wrote, with slight misrepresentation, for the YMCA's Tuxis Boys:

Some day you may have the glorious experience of climbing Maple Mountain, above Lady Evelyn Lake, Temagami, up the River Namabinnagasheshingue. In the joy of your youth and vigor you will revel not only in the beauties of that tiny trail, but will even glory in the portages, more than a score, which take from stretch to stretch, past falls and ledges varying from one foot to over one hundred feet in height, your camera ever busy to record the succession of scenes in unforgettable beauty.[1]

The oldest campers are now called Voyageurs, while the Pioneers are about fifteen years of age. Initially, all the older campers were called Pioneers and only the trip with the very oldest ones was co-ed. Now most of the trips are co-ed.

All four of the "Pioneer Co-ed," trips, from 1957 to 1960, left from Wanapitei's canoe docks on the Red Squirrel River, out onto Lake Temagami. Three travelled west and north up the Lady Evelyn River, with both of us as the leaders. The fourth trip, that of 1960, was led by Bruce and others as Carol was expecting our first child. All four trips were, in part, new for Wanapitei and, of course, new to us.

Our route for the 1959 trip was from Lake Temagami and the Lady Evelyn north across into the Arctic watershed and on down the rarely used Grassy-Mattagami rivers to Timmins. The historic route for both the Teme Augama Anishnabai and the fur traders north from Bear Island at the centre of Lake Temagami, where the Hudson's Bay Company (HBC) post existed from 1867 to 1971, was up the Red Squirrel and Anima Nipissing rivers, up the Montreal River and over the divide and down the Frederick House River to the Mattagami River and on to James Bay. The central portion of this route is now very congested and certainly not wilderness. Hence, we followed the more westerly route. Today, downstream from Timmins, even the Mattagami River itself is rather polluted and full of power dams and forest operations.

The 1960 trip, on a unique course from Lake Temagami to Lake

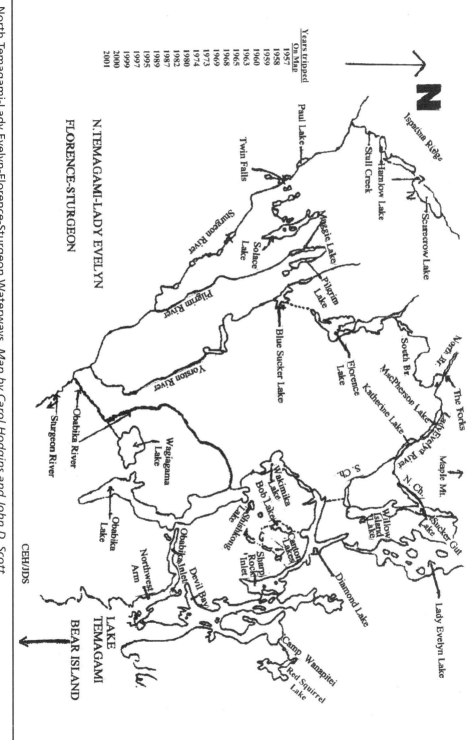

North Temagami-Lady Evelyn-Florence-Sturgeon Waterways. Map by Carol Hodgins and John D. Scott.

Wanapitei and then lake-hopping around the south of Sudbury and through the beautiful lakes to Killarney on north Georgian Bay, had probably not been paddled in the twentieth century, largely because the route around Sudbury had become so ugly, polluted and made barren from the sulphuric fumes.

All of these trips were paddled and portaged with white wood-canvas canoes, mostly sixteen feet long, mostly Chestnuts, Peterboroughs or Temagamis.[2] All of the canoes paddled out of Camp Wabanaki had been in wood-canvas. What else might one have used? We certainly did not use Grumman aluminum,[3] and very few people as yet used fibreglass. The old cedar-strip canoes were falling out of tripping use, and the birchbark canoe was long gone. We do, however, have a 1905 Temagami picture of American tourists. with local Teme-Augama Anishnabai guides and Father Charles Paradis[4] (who lived at what became the Wanapitei site), still all with birchbark canoes.[5] That was less than fifty years earlier.

The wood-canvas canoe was always heavier, both literally and figuratively, at the end of the voyage than at the beginning. Canoes were single-carried over portages, using both tied-in paddles and tump straps, those long leather straps with a headband in the centre. Used for portaging, the headband can take most of the weight of the canoe. That was the Temagami way. Many of the older and stronger females in the group joined in the single portaging of the canoes, but that was not yet either the Temagami or the general Canadian way. In the late fifties and early sixties few women single-carried canoes although they did carry heavy packs. Wanapitei was one of the first organizations where women and older girls single-carried their own canoes.

Large and rather heavy canvas tents provided protection from the elements, but we often slept under the stars if rain was not threatening. However, frequently we would be caught by a sudden deluge and then find ourselves having a dark, miserable and wet time of it, trying to put up the tents. To erect these tents, we used either ridge ropes or guy-line ropes, or a ridge pole and two front and two rear poles, lashed and spread out; the tents did not have floors.

Naturally, we cooked over an open, three-sided "Temagami-style" rock fireplace, using fresh green logs for the grate or grill. Can you believe it? Around 1960, the green logs were replaced by metre-long "fire irons." The environmental movement was underway! We slept in sleeping bags on groundsheets — no air mattress or foam pads. At first there was too much heavy canned food being carried in, although we did have a lot of spaghetti, with cheese and tomato paste, macaroni and Schneider's summer sausage. We would also rehydrate and cook up dehydrated potato flakes.

In 2000, Bruce wrote his article on the "Lady Evelyn River," published in Alistair Thomas's *Paddle Quest*:

> In haunting memory, the landscape of the Lady Evelyn keeps drawing me back for canoe voyages of both the imagination and the physical. Often more appropriately called the Trout Streams, its waters are as close to mountain flows as the Canadian Shield in Ontario can deliver. The Lady Evelyn has so many small, often unnavigable rapids, so many captivating high-yet-small falls, rugged Precambrian shorelines and heights, white and red pine stands, cedars, lily pads, shallows and depths, sunsets and portages, I simply must recanoe it and re-imagine its mysteries.[6]

In 1957, our route took us across Diamond Lake, over the long Barn Portage, (so-called because of the Murphy Lumber Barn that was once there) sleeping at night on top of two metres of soft hay. The barn is the now long gone. From there the route was up the South Channel of the Lady Evelyn, on up the main river past Macpherson Lake to the Forks, where the North and South Branch of the Lady Evelyn separated, then down the main channel and the North Channel, around Lady Evelyn Lake, and back across Diamond and Sharp Rock[7] to "home" under the bridge, amid a growing arrival ceremony at Wanapitei.

Of this trip Allie Fretz-Cressman wrote:

The second falls on the South Channel of the Lady Evelyn River.

In 1957 on the Co-ed Trip, I was a chaperone for about 12 of the oldest Pioneers, including unmarried leaders, Bruce and Carol. Soon I was carrying a 50 lb. pack, a new experience. It felt like about 100 lbs. As I had no canoe-tripping experience, the first portage presented a problem. I sat down to rest on a log and of course, overbalanced. I had to remain on my back, with the pack on top, until someone came along to rescue me—which seemed like forever. That evening we slept in "The Barn," on the hay, up the Lady Evelyn. Sometime during the night, I felt little tiny feet running over my head as I tried to get to sleep in my sleeping bag. I don't know who they were, but I have never forgotten it and always wondered.

The next morning we had pancakes for breakfast. I can't abide pancakes, so I decided to wait until lunch to eat. Lunch was eaten, after what seemed like an eternity, at two or three o'clock. Needless to say, I ate pancakes whenever they were available after that.

The next evening was cool, with a temperature of 42°F, so the guys built a good fire. Wayne Stevens' boots were wet, so he set them near the fire, toes first. They were good new boots, belonging to his Uncle Bert. The next morning, the boots were smoldering—and so was Wayne.

I still remember David Livingstone [a camper] carrying a canoe, which must have been as heavy as he was. The campers on this trip were marvellous. No one ever stepped out of line, and everyone worked as a team.[8]

In August 1958, we led the ten-day "Pioneer Co-ed" on the Makobe-Elk Lake Loop. The initial part of the route was the same as the Lady Evelyn Trip to Macpherson Lake in the Temagami District. We then struggled up the tiny Grays River and over a divide to the Makobe River, down its shallow (late August) waters with many carryovers, much wading and lining, and a few rapid shoots to the village of Elk Lake (of the silver boom fame) on the significant Montreal River. From there we paddled down the Montreal, with the Little Clay Belt northwest of New Liskeard on the left or southeast bank and Shield country on the right bank, and ran the Mountain Chutes (where we totally wrecked, in the shallow but large rapids, an old Archibald-era thirties wood-canvas canoe. Then after paddling far down the river, we portaged three kilometres into Anima-Nipissing Lake, down its full length, in and out of Carrying Lake, through Red Squirrel Lake and down its river to Camp Wanapitei.

On our honeymoon in July of that year we had, among other things, checked out the Makobe route from the Lady Evelyn to Elk Lake with old timers (loggers, trappers, and prospectors in Elk Lake). We did not know then of any written trip report covering the route, which strengthened its appeal for us.

In 1959, we paddled up the North Branch of the Lady Evelyn, close to its source at little Gamble Lake and took the very long portage up into and then down out of the clear, blue Sunnywater Lake, and on to Smoothwater Lake, a rather large lake near the top of the East Branch of the Montreal River. From there we descended that river north to Gowganda.

We next worked our way northwest, creek and lake-hopping via Houston Lake (where we picked up John Scott as further staff), and the Bigfour Lakes to a very long portage (ten kilometres) along a rough road over the divide, into the Arctic watershed and onto the Grassy River in northeastern Ontario. That night we camped on the island in Sinclair Lake, which contained a gorgeous stand of old growth pine. This site looked out on the mainland devastated by very heavily logged-over land, something close to what twenty years later we would call a "clear-cut." We passed by a very isolated Cree village, then followed down the swift Grassy River for another three days, paddling through Kapiskong Lake. While on that lake we used ground sheets, poles and paddles to sail north with the

Bruce in his tent at Houston Lake.

wind, until a one-minute absolute calm followed by a near gale and heavy rain from the north, made us cut the rigging and race for the shore. Later, we paddled between high clay banks until the Grassy emptied into the Mattagami River, which we descended to the southern outskirts of Timmins. After portaging through town with our canoes and attracting much attention, we took the Ontario Northland Railway to Goward (just north of Temagami village), and slept in the shack that served as the station. The next day we paddled and portaged westward on the difficult Kanichee-Jackpine "back route" to Red Squirrel Lake and back to the Camp. It was Wanapitei's first two-week trip.

In 1960, Bruce's co-leaders on the co-ed trip to Killarney on Georgian Bay, were Bonnie Gordon, Wayne Stevens, and for the second half, cousin Daryl Hodgins. It was a large group of over fifteen, unthinkable now.[9] In the beginning we paddled and portaged from Lake Temagami southwest across the Sturgeon River, then west through the northern Chiniguchi arc route to Lake Wanapitei, which had been the site of Camp Wanapitei in the Archibald days, from 1924 to 1930. The route as far as Lake Wanapitei had been traversed first in 1957 for the new Wanapitei regime "Pioneer Boy's Trip" led by Larry Hodgins, on advice from Ed Archibald.

From there we paddled down the middle section of the Wanapitei River, past Highway 17 just east of Sudbury. Further south, believe it or not, we lake-hopped westward around the city (past the old United Mine Workers camp and the present site of Laurentian University) to Lake Panache. From there, we took the now common route through the Killarney Mountains (Bell, Johnny, and George lakes etc.) to Georgian Bay, to Killarney village and its bay.

Here we stayed at Cecil and Marguerite Hodgins's (Daryl's parents) cottage site on Sheep Island. A great feature was a huge pork roast barbequed whole on a spit. Wow! Stan Hodgins (Bruce's father) and a car fleet hauled us back to Temagami for the long paddle back to the Camp. At the time we believed that it really was a unique route. Today, a Temagami-to-Killarney trip is a rather common one for Wanapitei, usually with thirteen- and fourteen-year-olds, but, so far, not with that strange arching paddle around Sudbury.

This trip was taken before the establishment of Killarney Provincial Park, before all the acid-rain and sulphur dioxide scares. We were conscious of the extra clear, high visibility in the water on many of the deeper Killarney Lakes — as we had with Sunnywater Lake in 1959. In areas such as these that were sustaining the wind drift from the Sudbury smelter stacks, the number of young lake trout was already in severe decline, if not already gone.

Canoeing through the Canadian Shield is rarely monotonous. It is so beautiful, especially where not damaged by severe overuse by humans. Yet two jewels, the Temagami Country and the Killarney Park and Georgian Bay coastline, are so different. The Killarney focus is on the high quartzite white hills, the cliffs and shorelines, and on the clear lakes. The Temagami-Lady Evelyn focus is on the deep water lakes, fast but small rivers, the ruggedness of the terrain, the granite ridges, and certainly the always endangered old growth, both the white and red pine trees.

# 2
## DOWN THE GRASSY-MATTAGAMI-MOOSE
## RIVERS TO JAMES BAY, 1961

The 1961 trip was Wanapitei's first "Bay Trip," a canoe voyage on the Grassy-Mattagami-Moose rivers to Moose Factory and Moosonee and onto James Bay. The first section (referred to as "Long Bays") was led by John Scott, the senior trip leader on the Wanapitei staff at the time. The route basically followed that set by Carol and Bruce in 1959 from Lake Temagami to Timmins, but with a haul over the divide.

After the changing of some staff, the group merged with the August "Co-ed Trip" led by Bruce and John, but this particular Co-ed had no females! The few eligible girls could not, at that time, secure parental approval for such a remote, and perhaps perceived as hazardous voyage. By 1971, parental attitudes would be so different, and the female teenagers so much more determined. However, many of the participants on the 1961 trip would go on to a lifetime of canoe tripping, and Ted Moores, one of the members of this trip, in particular would lead or organize dozens of far northern canoe trips for Wanapitei, for Outward Bound,[10] and just with friends.

For some one hundred kilometres paddling north on the Mattagami, the water was less than clean and pure — polluted by human and industrial waste, in this case from the gold mines and the Town of Timmins. Several existing chutes and rapids, bigger than any we had ever run before, may ultimately have purified the water. As we proceeded we noticed that even the shoreline and bush regained some splendour, demonstrated by the poplar and spruce stands of

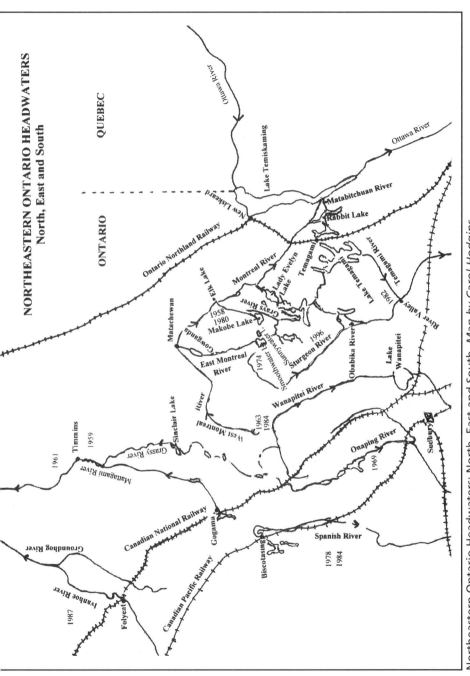

Northeastern Ontario Headwaters: North, East and South. *Map by Carol Hodgins.*

Scott LaRue and David Siebert shooting rapids on the Mattagami River.

the Clay Belt and the many Shield outcroppings. The trippers had to carry up and around the power dams and mill houses and Highway 11, at both Smooth Rock Falls and the existing dams found further north.

Continuing north, we encountered heavy dam construction for the Ontario James Bay power projects, causing us to take several carries and shoot many rough rapids. We passed Spruce Falls, Little Long and Long Rapids, all with dams or with ones being built. Finally, Grand Rapids ran free for three kilometres, wide and shallow, depositing us in the poorly drained James Bay Lowlands. Ahead would be more long stretches of wide class-one rapids running over gravel bars.

At the Cree community of Moose River Crossing, where the Ontario Northland Railway (ONR) crosses the Moose River, we all boarded the northbound train to buy ice cream cones. When the bell rang, signalling the train's departure, all but "Captain Bruce" got off before significant motion occurred. Bruce jumped down with one cone in each hand, one being for a camper. By this time the train was moving at a considerable speed and approaching the bridge. Over and over, he tumbled down the embankment. Amazingly, he stood up unscathed though humbled but with only the tiny dry bottoms of the cones in his hands.

After paddling on to Moose Factory and Moosonee, we camped at what, years later, would become Tidewater Provincial Park. We hired a Cree guide with his powered freight canoe and were driven out onto James Bay itself and back. Triumphantly, we took the mixed freight and passenger train, (the ONR's Little Bear) with the canoes, back to Goward, then paddled the Kanichee-Red Squirrel route back Wanapitei.

Since then Wanapitei has undertaken dozens of "Bay Trips," with Bruce and Carol leading only four of them, three being first runs for the Camp. Only one more Wanapitei trip that was  led by veteran trip leader Stuart Hunter in 1963 followed the Mattagami route. Regrettably, the Mattagami was no longer great canoe country, because of dams, pollution and roads and more roads in its upstream portion.

# 3

## EAST INTO NORTHERN QUEBEC; WEST INTO NORTHERN ONTARIO, 1962–68

Between 1962 and 1968 the annual two-week co-ed trips were led by Bruce and others, but not Carol because sons Shawn and Geoff were not yet old enough to be with Wanapitei campers. Instead, family day tripping and overnight trips together and with friends fulfilled the urge to be in canoes as paddling partners. In 1969, Carol was back and once more involved in the annual co-leadership.

The 1962 trip, like that of 1961, involved two linked voyages of two weeks each. Paul Richmond, a veteran camper and trip-leading staff person and still a friend today, and John Scott co-led with the six campers: Gordon Barrett, John Clarke, Tom Cobean, Carson Klinck, Ted Moores and Dale St. Clair. This was a long trip, paddling from Lake Temagami west across Lake Temiskaming, into Quebec and across the Lac Kipawa.

From there it was a lake-hopping journey past Grand Lake Victoria to Lac Dozois on the upper Ottawa River. At Lac Dozois, Bruce, along with Stuart Hunter, George Barrett, Cathy Squires, Sue McLeod and five female campers (including Jane Underhill and Ann Scott) replaced John Scott and several male campers, making a total of eighteen persons.

This large group paddled and portaged east across La Verendrye Reserve via the Cabonga Reservoir to the upper Gatineau, then south on that river all the way to the City of Ottawa. It was beautiful country, but with the river jammed so often with cut logs, travelling necessitated some truck hauls. Once they had

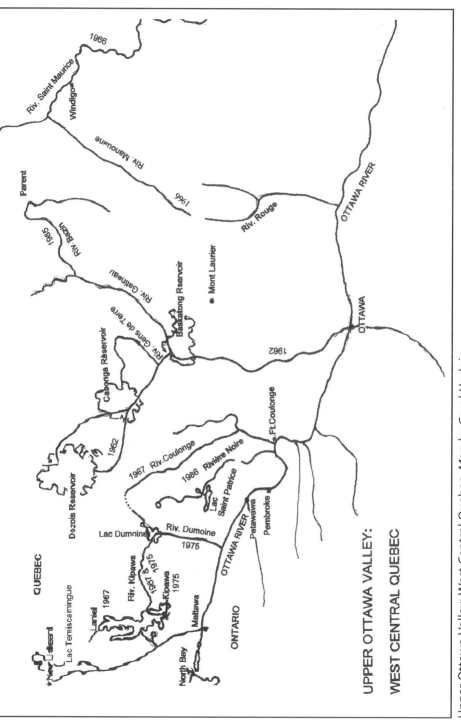

Upper Ottawa Valley: West Central Quebec. *Map by Carol Hodgins.*

crossed the lower Ottawa River, camp was set up by the mouth of the Rideau River, on its east bank near the French Embassy and close to 24 Sussex Drive, the residence of the prime minister (then John Diefenbaker).

After having toured the capital, the group continued their paddle across the Ottawa River, up to the northern outlet of the Rideau Canal, the group portaged up to and across Rideau Street by the Chateau Laurier to the old Central Station. The trip back to Camp Wanapitei was first by train to Goward (just north of Temagami) and from there the paddling and portaging resumed along the traditional Kanichee-Red Squirrel route. Many are still friends, forty-five years later!

In 1963, automobiles (with trailers) hauled the annual co-ed Wanapitei trip from Temagami north and west to Gogama, west of Elk Lake and north of Sudbury. With Bruce as their leader, the group put in on the Minisinakwa River (of the Mattagami-James Bay watershed). The route took them paddling downstream and then up the Nabakwasi and Opikinimika rivers, south over the great north-south divide and onto Meteor Lake. For a week we paddled down the full upper Wanapitei River, across its lake and then took the complex Chiniguchi route pioneered by brother Larry Hodgins (in 1956) northeast to Lake Temagami—quite a unique three-sided course.

The next year, 1964, Bruce was so occupied with the completion of his doctoral dissertation that we only paddled day trips. Ted Moores and others led two linked, long co-ed trips west over water and over land to Searchmount, north of Sault Ste. Marie and almost to Lake Superior.

Bruce, Ted Moores and Joyce Leckie led the co-ed trip in 1965, up the full northwestern waters of the Lady Evelyn to Florence Lake. From there, they portaged and lake-hopped west to the Sturgeon River at the tiny Ghoul Lake, almost straight west of Florence. The group descended the Sturgeon for five full days of rapids, waterfall and long fast paddles, right to the base of the Obabika system and east up its river, creeks and lakes to Lake Temagami. This was a truly great circle route in Northern Ontario's *pays d'en haut*. The route is now paddled most years by rugged groups from Wanapitei and several other youth camps and adult outfitters.

In 1966, there was another set of linked trips. Bruce and other Camp Wanapitei leaders were responsible for the innovative second half. Once again Ted Moores took his section east from Temagami through Quebec's La Verendrye Reserve and then at nearby Camp Nominingue he joined up with Bruce and the co-ed component, which had been driven to the site by station wagons. From nearby the group paddled north on the Rouge watercourse, over the divide from the Ottawa onto the St. Maurice watershed, and down the long and remote Manouane River to the St. Maurice River at the tiny village of Sanmaur. From this point the short distance to the complete ghost town of Wendigo, an abandoned lumber and hydroelectric community, was by train, necessitated by the extra fast and log-infested high water of a late season "sweep" (the practice of pulling and floating the logs of the shallow water and shoreline, usually by power boat).

Then it was onward downstream to the south, paddling through monstrous log jams and once carried on corporate-supplied tug boats, past La Tuque to Mattawin (not far above Shawinigan Falls)

Poling through a log jam.

where family vehicles met the group and hauled everyone back the long way to Temagami. The group had been very large and many individuals had tripped with Wanapitei before. Trip staff such as Allan Norris and Ann Scott were very important to Wanapitei in the future, and they continue to be our friends.

In 1967, Centenary Year, the great co-ed trip was on the Quebec's Coulonge River, a river flowing into the Ottawa below the Dumoine and once famous for its lumbering and its log runs. The group led by Bruce, Ted Moores and Carlene Ridley, put in at the village of Laniel on Lac Kipawa and paddled the now usual lake-hopping route east to Lac Dumoine. Then it was upstream on La Rivière Orignal and over the remote divide, helped by a haul from some by lumber trucks working in the vicinity, to the source of the Coulonge River. From

Shawn, Bruce, Geoff and Carol Hodgins hiking in Temagami at Wanapitei, c. 1968.

here (Lac Pompone) the paddlers descended the full Coulonge to its Grand Rapids, just upstream from Fort Coulonge, once a North West Company fort and now a thriving village on the Ottawa. Most of the group were then driven back to Temagami—though a few went the other way to take in the excitement of Expo 67.

The 1968 co-ed trip from Temagami was led by Bruce and others, past Lake Wanapitei, to Killarney, on a radically different route south of Sudbury from that of the 1960 trip. From Lake Panache, the route took the trippers southwest on the so-called Whitefish River (really a series of linked lakes) to Whitefish Falls and ultimately to Iroquois Bay of Georgian Bay. Paddling eastwards, the group entered and left Kirks Creek (in Killarney Park), and finally into Killarney, OAS and George lakes and back onto Georgian Bay to Killarney. This was a beautiful route, especially in the Killarney area with its rugged mountains, rocky shores and clear deep lakes though many would not relish the electric power developments on the middle Wanapitei River, nor the many cottages and motor boats on the Whitefish section.

# 4.

## WESTWARD TO BEAUTY LAKE, SHOOFLY LAKE, SCOTIA LAKE AND THE ONAPING RIVER, 1969

By 1969 Carol was back into the adventuresome tripping. With the co-ed group we undertook a unique but marvellous route from Lake Temagami west to the northern source (Beauty Lake) of the Lady Evelyn River. From there we obtained a short truck haul northwest to Opikinimika Lake, in the James Bay watershed, then back south over the north-south divide to Shoofly Lake on the upper reaches of the Wanapitei River. Our route continued over hill, dale and swamp to Scotia Lake, the upper Onaping River, and down it all the way to Levack, where time ran out. From Levack we chartered a school bus to take us southeast and north to Emerald Lake, whence we paddled north to Obabika Lake, Temagami Lake, and ultimately "home."

That year we had a very large group. Patricia Irwin, Diane Gauthier and Dale St. Clair formed the staff along with the two of us and John Clarke and Catherine Wilson joined us part way through the trip. Included among the campers were Marcus Bruce, Gary Norris, Shelley Beal, Catherine Falmagne, Diane Forbes, Lynn Palliser, Colin Campbell, Jon Cole, Pierre Gauthier, Paul Hartley, Al King, Bill Rosman and Alistair Thomas. Alistair has since written and edited several canoeing books and several of these young canoeists would become lifelong friends and associates. Some excerpts from our logs or trip reports provide interesting insights into the texture of our time together:

> August 8, Day 1:
> …For us, paddling against head winds was soon

to become a pattern of the trip. When we were travelling north we generally had a north wind to face; when we were travelling south we generally faced a south wind. We had the wind against us as we paddled through Sharp Rock Inlet and through Diamond Lake to the two mile portage and then to Willow Island Lake. Before we reached that Lake we withstood a 10-minute downpour. The portage itself was extremely muddy. The short downpour only added a little bit of surface water along the trail. The day before the trip the Temagami area had withstood its heaviest rain and thunderstorm of the season. That storm, we were later to learn, had, in fact, produced a small twister, which had knocked over the Bear Island fire tower and cut a swath through the islands, just missing Friday's Camp. It had knocked down hundreds of trees.... We camped on the site of the old [Murphy Lumber] Barn, no longer there. We had a dinner of fried potatoes, fresh hamburger, peas and pineapple cake.

Bruce lining up the Lady Evelyn River.

August 13, Day 6:
Up at 8 a.m. Away (to the south). We arrived at Lake Opikinimika at 10:15. Intermittent drizzle. Overcast sky. We paddled the six miles of the Lake while Bruce, Diane, Marcus, Dale and others delivered renditions. We then took the rather simple portage over the north-south continental divide, out of the Arctic Watershed back into the St. Lawrence [Georgian Bay] Watershed and into Meteor Lake, which is Wanapitei River water. This Lake is much more pleasant than the brushy, flat shore of Opikinimika. Meteor has bluish water and several islands, lots of loons, and a small number of rock outcroppings....

August 14, Day 7:
Up at 8:15 a.m. Away at 10:15, portaging into a puddle south of Shoofly Lake. We then entered a creek and finally paddled through a great mess of windfall and driftwood, breaking into the upper Wanapitei River above a portage. It would probably be better to portage into Oshawong Lake and then proceed directly up the River, which here is little more than a creek. After some pull-ups we made a 300 yard portage on the left, cutting into a main trail bypassing the pull-ups themselves. Then we pushed up to the CNR Bridge, where we stopped for a little break, then pushed on and into Kalaco Lake. We were happy now to be in country that Wanapitei personnel had never travelled before. We paddled from Kalaco into Kamenisa, and then continued up the Wanapitei River. We had lunch on a portage on the right in a Jack pine grove at 2:30. We had one short portage and then reached an old dilapidated log jam at the north end of Scotia Lake. This we lifted over and began paddling south against a strong south wind. The Lake which is about twelve miles long is a truly

superb one, with high rock banks and heavy forest, but it is shy on campsites.

About four miles down the Lake we stopped on the west or right side; here is a good rock ledge that could conceivably serve as a campsite for a small group. We had a roaring fire and cooked a huge dinner of pizza and cake. Because this was not a site for twenty persons, we pushed on at 8:45 p.m. with the wind dying down. As darkness fell, we continued to the south, until we saw a light on the west shore. This turned out to be from the only cabin on Scotia Lake, one owned by the Sudbury Aviation Company. Here were four fishermen from Brantford, workers from the Massey-Ferguson plant. They were glad to see us and most hospitable. Soon they were serving coffee to all twenty of us. That night eight slept in two tents. Carol and Bruce slept under the stars, and ten persons slept on the floor of the cabin. At dusk it had cleared to a cloudless night with no bugs....

Camping at Emerald Lake in the Obakika (Temagami area) on the return trip.

August 17, Day 16:

We were up at 8:00 a.m. for what turned out to be the highlight day of the trip. Away at 10:15. The rapids were to be shot on the difficult set, by the campsite, without middlemen, after giving it considerable study. Then a simple set and a complex one (where Bruce broke his paddle), we portaged around the falls, "marked rapids," on the map. We shot two more sets, than the second, marked as "falls" on the map. We shot many more sets, and then we met three fishermen from Levack. They had hiked up from the village and were camped further down the River….

For us it was great to be paddling partners on a two-week-long trip and as the senior leaders with a group of experienced young canoeists.

# PART TWO:

# THE ADVENTURESOME SEVENTIES, 1970–1979

# 5
## ROUND THE WORLD AND ACROSS FOUR CONTINENTS, 1970

I n late November 1969, with our two boys, Shawn, almost nine, and Geoff, seven, we flew from Montreal to Shannon, Ireland. Our newly purchased bright red Westphalia Volkswagen Camper was waiting on the tarmac. Our adventuresome round-the-world trip began. We spent a month in Europe having Christmas in Copenhagen, Denmark, with Carol's sister and family, who were living there at the time.

New Year's Eve, welcoming in the seventies, found us in a small motel outside Zagreb (Croatia) celebrating with the manager, and with a young attractive actress and her salesman boyfriend. We were joined by two Yugoslavian soldiers on patrol duty. Their rifles with long bayonets were placed across our table. We wonder if any of them survived the bloody strife that lay ahead in the now vanquished Yugoslavia.

Wherever we were driving, we often read about the history of each area; the boys loved it. Having children was an advantage. People were generally very friendly and fascinated by our two, then, very blond boys. However, the long formal process at some borders was very bureaucratic and sometimes took a couple of hours.

Upon reflection, our experiences were many and memorable. They range from the impressive architecture of Turkey to Bruce being arrested in Afghanistan between Kandahar and Kabul for innocently driving through an unmarked toll chain across the road. Fortunately, this situation was rectified amicably. Among our many memories are

**Top**: "The Taj Mahal in India, with only the four of us in view." **Bottom**: Camping in the Nullabar Plain in southwestern Australia, during the drive from Perth to Canberra.

the shock of entering the Khyber Pass to find armed guards at every curve in the road and the amazing contrasts in India and the beauty of Ceylon (now Sri Lanka). The list could go on.

Living in Australia gave us the opportunity to make many friends, and even to do some paddling together on the continent's rivers. On one excursion we actually stood on the Australian shore where Captain James Cook had first sighted the land exactly two hundred years before.

We spent five months based in Canberra where Bruce had an appointment at the Australian National University. When his appointment was completed, we flew across the Pacific Ocean, and our camper van was sent across ahead of us by freighter. However, en route back to Peterborough, we  first took time to experience New Zealand, then went back to Sydney. From there we flew home, making stops in Bali and Singapore and on to Japan where we went to Expo 70 in Osaka.

Finally we were in Vancouver, back on Canadian soil still treasuring our memories. This around the world trip will always remain a never-to-be-forgotten voyage, an educational experience of changing landscapes and various cultures, with many wonderful albeit brief encounters with so many people, along with the making of new friends.

# 6

## THE LOWER ALBANY TO JAMES BAY, 1971

In each of the years, 1971 and 1972, we led co-ed youth trips with sixteen- and seventeen-year-olds, to James Bay. The beautiful but rather easy route taken in 1971 was on the Nagagami and Kenogami rivers and on the lower Albany River, down to the Cree community of Fort Albany. There were twenty of us, including Allan (Vin) Norris and Shelley Beal who were on staff at Wanapitei again. Campers included many future staff members, shareholders and future parents of campers, including Hilary Heath and Gary Norris.

After the first day the paddle was all north of the Canadian Shield, making our way through the James Bay Lowlands, with the boreal spruce woods thinning out and growing smaller as we approached salt water. Our canoes were rather old wood-canvas ones, made weaker as they bumped and scraped over the wide gravelly shallows, springing many leaks as we made our way. Heated spruce pitch and gum, and much bailing, were needed to make our destination, where we were immediately made honorary participatory guests in an almost all-night community square dance.

We sold two of the most heavily-repaired canoes for next to nothing, knowing that the Cree could secure free canvas for canoe recovering from Indian Affairs. As for the remainder of the canoes, we had to pay for shipping them out by barge and then by train back to Temagami. We flew out to Moosonee on a single-engine Otter on pontoons and from there boarded the Ontario Northland train south to Temagami.

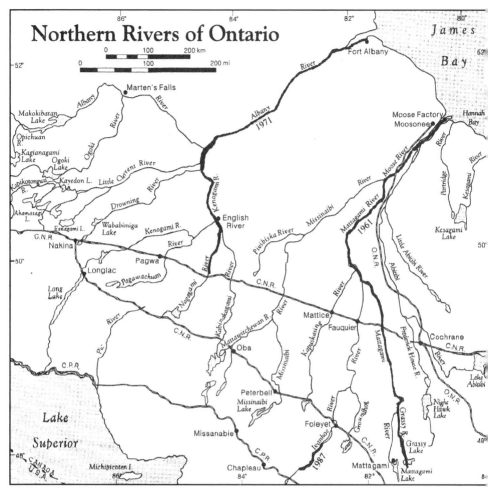

Northern Rivers of Ontario. *From* Canoeing North into the Unknown, *30.*

From the our log comes our first-hand experience of this paddling experience:

> Day 12, Wednesday:
> Up at 7:30 to a clear sky. Away at 10:15 against a northeast wind. Shallow light rapids. We had lunch at 2:00 on the gravel on the south side by the first island of the Albany River's estuary. We followed a course along the south side, through some unmarked swifts just before the long island (the second of the estuary),

Our first campsite en route to Fort Albany.

and over the marked rapids by the small third island. Over the second marked set between the south shore and island), various patches on No. 40 [canoe] were ripped off. We built a large fire and gathered spruce gum—luckily Tine Sivell found an old can for boiling, in it was some old dried tar. This we heated, and together with the spruce gum patched and tarred the bottom. This sealed up the leaks until the gum was later chipped off on the gravel beds. We also repaired No. 45. We left at 7:00 p.m., proceeding along the channels to Sinclair Island; they were extremely shallow and the canoes scraped a lot.

The narrow three-mile channel between Sinclair and the south shore, leading directly to the village of Fort Albany was virtually upon us, we had to steer around the large island. Huge thunder clouds were building up to the northwest. As the storm neared we pulled up on the shore two-thirds of the way along Sinclair. It was pitch dark with loud thunder and lightning but virtually no rain. The storm passed.

There was muskeg everywhere and no open sites. With only two miles to go, we decided to push on. One boat was now leaking very badly and had to be dumped frequently, despite bailing. We could not navigate the channel between Sinclair and the little island to its north-east, so round we went. Still no sign of life. Then we paddled on to the south, back to Sinclair and found the narrow passage between it and Anderson Island.

Butch [Gary] Norris noted a "channel marker," then several more. They turned out to be buoyed plastic outboard cans. Then we passed power lines. Then a dark freight canoe was sited and then dozens of canoes on the shore. Then over the top of the high bank we saw a church steeple. Landing, we climbed the bank and saw what looked like a totally sleeping village (pop. 500). The Cree were not asleep; most everyone was off at the Rec. Hall seeing a western trio, "Smilin' Johnny," flown in for stage shows. Five of us walked past the high steepled church on a dusty road down over a causeway to the mainland site of the Oblate Mission (hospital, school, etc.). Finally we saw Frère Alex Gagnon who quickly became a great friend. Soon this tri-lingual brother had us outfitted with food, including fresh-baked bread hot from the oven of the resident Cree baker (who like most other older inhabitants spoke only Cree). Alex took us back to the main group in his old jeepster. Others there had made contact with Chris Merriman, manager of the Hudson's Bay Post, opposite our landing spot on Anderson Island (also joined by a causeway). Alex arranged with a Cree, Peter Sackaney for us to stay (sleep), after the concert at the Rec. Hall, which he runs.

There we heard that a square dance would follow the concert, so Alex took us back to the

Leaving Fort Albany by float plane.

mission where we had lunch with hot chocolate. About 9:00 p.m. we went to the Rec. Hall, only to find the dance in full swing. Depositing our packs in Peter Sackaney's house we joined with the square dance to the great glee of the locals. (Tine fell asleep on the pounding floor of the Hall.) At 3:15 am the dance ended, but "Smilin' Johnny" didn't want us sleeping with his expensive audio equipment. So we were all billeted with the Sackaneys' and their friend Johnny Roderick.

The Albany trip was a great voyage and an enlightening experience. The River, however, was frequently too shallow and hard on the bottoms of wood-canvas canoes. The Cree at Fort Albany were so hospitable and rather wonderful in making us feel welcome.

# 7
## THE WASWANIPI-BROADBACK-RUPERT RIVERS, QUEBEC, 1972

The next year found us co-leading, with Marcus Bruce and Gay Wadham, the second and harder portion of an end-to-end challenging and memorable canoe trip from Lake Temagami to Rupert House (now Waskaganish) on the Quebec shore of James Bay, at a large Cree community that began as a major Hudson's Bay Company Post in the 1670s. Marcus and Allan Norris led the first half, east to Lake Temiskaming, then upstream in Quebec and north on the Upper Ottawa and its tributaries, over the historic Arctic divide and down the Bell (upper Nottaway) River to Matagami. Here we, with several staff and campers, met them. Once again some from the first section of the trip returned to camp.

Once reassembled with our nineteen campers and four leaders, we paddled east along the full length of Matagami Lake and up the Waswanapi River to Lac Evans, over to the Broadback River. We continued down the river for several days to the old fur-trade Rupert Carry to Lac Nemiscou. We stayed overnight in the old HBC post of Nemiscou, recently abandoned when it was assumed that the Rupert River, when dammed, would flood Nemiscou.

The trip was caught in the midst of the great controversies concerning the beginnings of Hydro Quebec's massive plans to dam up many of the large rivers flowing into James Bay on the Quebec side. Initially, this was to focus on the Rupert and the Broadback rivers. Unlike in Ontario, the Quebec Cree had not been treated by the Federal Crown. They resisted. Later a tripartite agreement was worked out, and the huge La

Hanging fish filets in the village of Rupert House, now known as Waskaganish.

Grande watershed was harnessed first. Now, in its third phase, plans are underway again to divert some of the waters of the upper Rupert to the north through the Eastmain and into La Grande.

From there we took the shorter Link Route from Nemiscou off the main channel of the Rupert. Now back on the main river, we paddled down its many rapids and portaged around its many falls (especially Oatmeal Falls) where the James Bay Highway now crosses the River, to Rupert House. Here we were royally treated by the recently elected young Cree Chief Billy Diamond.[1] We were given accommodations in the teachers' house as no one was there for the summer. Later we flew south on a Canso Flying Boat back to Matagami. Because of problems noted below, we were a few days late in reaching the Wanapitei home base.

Earlier as we were approaching Oatmeal Falls we still did not know that work had already begun on the northern Quebec Highway for the huge James Bay Hydroelectric Project. We, Carol and Bruce, were taken up in a helicopter to see the construction of a major bridge at the Falls.

What follows are two days of reports from our log:

August 13, Day 13:
Up at 5:45 a.m. Cold and misty with some of the

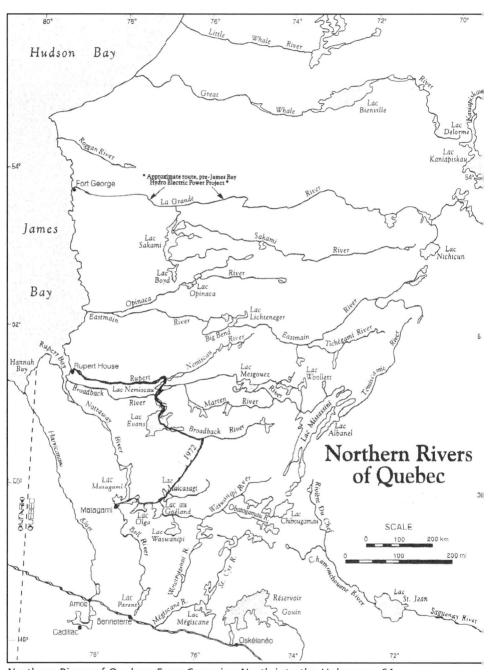

Northern Rivers of Quebec. *From* Canoeing North into the Unknown, *64.*

N.W. wind continuing. Away at 7:00 a.m. after cinnamon rolls for breakfast. We paddled up Gifford Lake as the mist began to clear, picking our way among the many islands keeping basically to the western side. The portage around the rapids-falls complex, on the Broadback begins on the left in a reedy bay, just after one can see the spray from the top of the first pitch. The carry is one mile long, beginning at a flat rock around the reeds and tag alders. After the first 100 yards, the trail is excellent. (Another version probably begins at the head of the reedy bay, but it was too shallow to reach.) On the trail was a campsite and an Indian cemetery. Back on the River the sky cleared as we paddled down the 3 miles to the beginning of the Broadback-Rupert Carry. The Carry begins on a stony site where the River turns west and where a minor branch from Gifford Lake enters the main stream.

Lunch at noon. Noticed a single set of footprints on the trail, perhaps a day old. Portage began at 12:45. Carol and John Tevlin over at 2:30 and the first canoes at 3:10. Nancy Barootes and Paul Marshall had some trouble. Marcus, Gay, Sherry Shiff and Bruce went back. Last ones over at 5:30. A lot of muskeg on first 1/3, and the last 100 yards are over a mushy open moose marsh to a short tiny deep creek, which flows into Wettigo Lake. Total distance of portage is 3½ miles. Some canoes paddled ahead across the 2½ miles of Wettigo. The carry out of Wettigo is 100 yards. leaving from the top of the clogged outlet creek. Some muskeg on the first part. It was a 3 mile paddle from there to the village of Nemiscou. The Hudson's Bay Post had closed in 1970, and the Cree village was totally abandoned. The last of us arrived at 8:45 p.m. Jo Wallich, a Quebec geologist, and his Cree assistant were staying at the Post but were out at work on our arrival, but Skip Porter was there. He had arrived in the morning. An ex-Wabun staff member, who had tripped the River twice, was on a solo trip from Lake Mistassini on the Marten-Rupert River route. Glad at last to be on the Rupert ourselves, we settled in, sleeping on the floor of the old Hudson's Bay store. After the geologists returned, we used their propane stove and ate in their building, the old warehouse. Jo gave us quite a bit of food for the extra three days of our trip which now, obviously, lay ahead. Dinner of baked meat pie and cake. Talked late. These were the first people we had seen since the trip began. High morale.

August 15, Day 15:

Cold and clear although heavy mist for an hour. Light frost during the night. We later learned that the temperature had dipped to at least 32°F. It warmed quickly while we had a slow pancake breakfast. Away at 9:00, but Sue Hahn, who had lost her knapsack, had to go back with Paul Marshall to the last portage on the Link to recover it. Marcus and his bowsperson Hilary Heath waited for them. The rest shot through a mile-long horserace [a long stretch of very fast-moving water] and into a wide stretch of the river. Beautifully clear and warm weather as we glided over perfectly clear water. We examined and shot on the left the marked rapids at the start of the large island we had just passed on the south. With the trip re-united, we ate lunch on a little beach 200 yards beyond.

Paddling on, we shot the swift at the end of the island and another along the second island. During this period we were surprised to see DC3s (land planes) disappear for landings beyond the trees to the south. Then we saw lots of helicopter activity. Just before the horserace above Oatmeal Falls we were buzzed by a helicopter. Then it landed on the north shore beside us. Bob, the American pilot just back from Viet Nam, asked us if we needed anything. He flew Carol and Bruce into the modern construction camp made up of trailers pulled up on a winter road. Carol and Bruce wired Temagami, reporting our good health but late progress, and they received some fresh food. The camp, run by BOT Construction, was engaged in building a portion of the then dubbed Fort George Highway which is to cross the Rupert just below Oatmeal Falls. To date, the roadbed was cleared to a point about two miles north of the River with construction crews further up the line for 15 miles. The bridge work had not commenced but a barge carried heavy equipment and men across the river between the horserace and the falls. So urgent was the construction that turboprop helicopters were airlifting 45-gallon gas drums and other supplies in slings to the road-head to save time. The pilot flew Bruce and Carol back to the group and then took Carol, the new food and two heavy packs and Skip to the surveyors' campsite 300 yards below the end of the portage. Skip returned.

We paddled the horserace right along the north shore and swung into a little creek on the River, just before the rocks at the head of the cascade. The portage, leaving from a pool on the creek, is 1200 yards long, over a very good trail. Pilot Bob, with Mr. Bot on an inspection tour, buzzed us repeatedly as the group wound snake-like through the dense forest. The trail led us out onto the wide area cleared for the highway, where we stopped and viewed this most impressive of northern falls from the cliff edge. All of us hoped it would never disappear into a dam site. The trail was tricky where the edge of the road had obliterated the route. Over an old campsite now destroyed at the end, we put into the current and whitehorses and paddled the 300 yards to the campsite which was reached at 6:15 p.m. Carol had the fire made beside the shore, and we put up tents high up on the plateau above the cliffs. Dinner of hamburg and steak, lettuce, canned tomatoes and little cakes. Later Bob returned by helicopter with two other pilots, staying until dark and bringing everyone pop. They flew off about 10:00 p.m.

The bad weather and the unexpected difficulties on the trip had caused us to fall behind schedule. We phoned home so Wanapitei and families would not worry. All arrived back safely.

# 8

## THE LADY EVELYN RIVER AND
## THREE EASTERN RIVERS, 1973

In July 1973, Carol and Bruce had their first experience with leading an adult (both male and female) canoe trip. We were transported by vehicles from Temagami via Elk Lake to a bush road (soon to be called the Liskeard Road) and ultimately to a launching spot near the Forks of the Lady Evelyn River. Our route found us paddling down the North Branch and North Channel, then over to Maple Mountain. We then returned back to Lake Temagami. The participants in this venture were Margo and Jim Fawcett, Carol and Jim Lemon and Barbara Truax.

What follows are the log reports for Day 2 and Day 3, the latter involving the climbing of Maple Mountain:

> Tuesday, Day 2:
> Up at 7:00 a.m. Clear sky. Away at 9:00 behind a Camp Wabun trip. Looking left down the first set of rapids which we shot—good run. We also shot the second set and the brief third one into Divide or Katherine Lake. We proceeded down the North Channel, portaging the first set on the north side (35 yds), which had a hill at the end. We met another Wabun group going upstream. Paddled down to Helen's Falls where we met two Sudbury couples going upstream. We weaved our way through its rocks and boulders. It was very hot. We rested, had

lunch then completed the portage. Swam below the falls; saw a water snake. In the afternoon shot one set before Centre Falls; rested halfway across the portage and put feet in the water. Completed the portage over the boardwalk and steeply tiled strata. We then paddled to Frank's Falls. We left our canoes on the upper end, portaged across with our gear to the campsite on high ground 20 yds from the lower end, 8:00 p.m. We had a good view of the falls. Dinner of soup and pizza. Mosquitoes at dusk. Bed at 10:15.

Wednesday, Day 3:
Up at 7:00 a.m. Away at 9:00, Hazy. Paddled down the Channel to Sucker Gut Lake, through the swamp area into Willow Island Creek. Reached the second (and better) campsite in Hobart Lake at 11:40. It was hot and muggy. Canoe repair, lunch and rest. Paddled into Tupper Lake with empty canoes.

Our group hiked to the top of Maple Mountain in the Temagami area. This is the second highest spot in Ontario.

> Arrived at the landing at 4:00; climbed Maple
> Mt., taking about two hours. Trail muddy in lower
> reaches; then up and down over several ridges, then
> up the final face. Picked blueberries on top. Some
> climbed the [fire] tower. Good view, but somewhat
> hazy. The descent took a little over an hour. Reached
> our campsite about 9:00 p.m. Dinner of meat pie;
> bed 10:30.

As mentioned, this was the first adult trip that we led. We found it an exhilarating experience and most of the participants would later return for more. Soon these adult trips would extend much further into the North and be more adventuresome and longer in duration. But we would repeatedly return to the beautiful Lady Evelyn watershed.

In August 1973, Bruce, along with Cathy Fretz, Tom McCullough and Claudette Languedoc led a large twenty-three-person, youth co-ed trip on three eastern rivers: the Matapedia in Quebec to New Brunswick, the Southwest Miramichi in New Brunswick and the short West River to Charlottetown, Prince Edward Island. (Carol declined to go because she felt there were too many people for one canoe trip). This would be the last Wanapitei canoe trip with such a large group.

An excerpt from the log concerning the Matapedia provides some insight into this experience:

> Day Two: Canoeing on the Matapedia River, Quebec
>     Away at 9:15 a.m. Shot a three-foot falls, which
> had a smooth passage on left. All morning we
> paddled, shooting light and medium rapids and swifts.

High spirits. Lunch by a roadside picnic site by the mouth of Rivière Froid. In the afternoon the River got even faster; it was like one great, glorious shelf. High hills. Beautiful countryside. Then we reached Assemetquagan Falls (really a complex rapids over limestone ridges); this took two hours to portage and shoot. Then we shot more rapids and swifts, paddling under the bridge between Matapedia at St. Laurent and entered the Restigouche River. We landed in a maple grove owned by the local Salmon Club. Secured permission to camp. A lot of fishermen in the River, using very thick canvas covered V-stern Chestnuts. Arrived in the village. This turned out to be our best day. Car drivers took 9:00 p.m. train back to Amqui for vehicles.

We, Carol and Bruce, had often driven along parts of the Matapedia on our frequent runs between Ontario and Prince Edward Island and we revelled in its beauty and paddleable whitewater.

Poling on the Miramichi River in New Brunswick.

The complex Miramichi is one of the largest watersheds in New Brunswick. It is very important for salmon fishing and the timber in its vicinity,

The West River came up only while the group was paddling on the Miramichi. We decided then that the logging politics and the shallowness of the River were conflicting with our tripping enjoyment. So, we decided to drive to the Island and paddle on this River for the remaining time—a good decision.

While we would plan and outfit many more co-ed Voyageur Youth Trips for Wanapitei, our own trip leading would henceforth be with adults.

# 9

## DOWN THE UPPER STURGEON RIVER, 1974

In July 1974, we were paddling partners once more, co-leading an adult trip on the upper Sturgeon. Some of the participants on the trip were Margo and Jim Fawcett, Dorothy and Ron Sears, Barbara and Art Truax, and Louise Rohanczy.

To reach our put-in point, we were driven north along the bush route from Temagami (via Elk Lake) to the upper (southern) bridge on the East Branch of the Montreal River. Once there we paddled south over the north-south divide and past the Ishpatina Ridge (highest peak in Ontario at 692 metres—the slopes are heavily forested with old growth white pine interspersed with granite ridges). Snare Creek was bypassed by means of a long carry on an old logging road that took us to the upper Sturgeon.

For a week we paddled down the Sturgeon River, over to the Obabika River and Lake and back to Lake Temagami. Water levels on the Sturgeon were quite high, and with a few of the participants we were, perhaps, "pushing the envelope." All were cooperative but the less experienced found the physical and canoeing requirements a little too challenging. Nevertheless, reassured, they carried on.

About two-thirds of the way down a portion of the Sturgeon, as we were paddling, Jim Lemon, our only middleman (one who is not paddling), suddenly and without considering the consequences, grabbed a large overhanging branch. In a flash, over went the canoe and an immediate rescue was required. Later, in the same canoe, sternsman Al Gamble lost his balance, and thinking he was going to tip the canoe, miraculously did a back flip out of it. Carolyn Lemon was in the bow and unaware of his gymnastics, as she was enjoying herself and concentrating on her canoeing and the narrow river ahead. She continued paddling the canoe down a relatively modest but long set of rapids. No one was in danger, the rescue was well-handled and everyone had a good laugh.

# 10

## THE KIPAWA AND THE DUMOINE, QUEBEC, 1975

Apaddling trip to the east of Temagami was our focus for 1975. We put in at Kipawa Village, Quebec. The site had once been a small Hudson's Bay Post with a significant Algonquin community nearby. In time it became a lumbering settlement with over nineteen lumber companies owning limits around the lake. Today, the village is at the terminal of a CPR spur line and like Temagami it is an embarkation point for travel by small boats and canoes into a complex lake and river system to the east.

We took the lake-hopping route east to Lac Dumoine and then spent a fun-filled week descending that great but, at that time, still remote Near North whitewater river down to the Ottawa. We paddled across the Ottawa River to the Ontario side where we had our pick-up. Participants on this venture were: Dick and Dawna Armstrong, Jim and Margo Fawcett, Al Gamble, Alma Norman, Louise Rohanczy, Ron and Dorothy Sears. Much of the excitement of this trip is captured in this selection from our log:

> July 22, Day 7:
> Up at 6:30 a.m. Two more canoes were shot through the rapids and the first two canoes were portaged over the next falls by Jim Fawcett and Bruce who singled the following swifts with light gear and then portaged the third falls. The rest followed. Dick Armstrong had some trouble with the last canoe in the rapids, but

Canoes on the Kipawa Lake-Dumoine River trip in Quebec.

by 9:40 all people and packs were at the foot of the complex, ready for the 1½ mile horserace into Little Italy Lake. Then we shot the threefold set and, after study, shot the fourth with light gear, taking in water. We ate lunch at its base. After lunch we portaged two sets (the first with a rough trail) and shot another, the one with an abandoned smashed fibreglass canoe in it. Bruce and Carol got stuck on a rock, and Louise Rohanczy, in the middle, had to get out. With the canoe freed, Louise waded and then floated down to the bottom of the set. Then we had six sets of major rapids. Examining each, we shot the first three, let down the fourth on the left, and shot the long fifth on the far left after a centre start. Al Gamble and Louise ran aground after not making the turn; we shot the sixth, involving a right circle route through an eddy (to view what was ahead) and back across the current, whereas some of those following made a very hard left turn and shot right through. We camped on the left, about one-half mile downstream at 5:00 p.m. It rained hard for a while. Early to bed.

This was Wanapitei's fourth trip on the exciting and ever popular Dumoine River, the first with adults. The youth trips usually begin in Temagami, paddling down the Matabitchewan, across Lake Temiskaming, up to Lac Kipawa and over to the Dumoine. As we discovered, the Dumoine is a very scenic river and very suited to teaching whitewater paddling. Our group loved it.

# 11
## ON THE SOUTH NAHANNI RIVER, NORTHWEST TERRITORIES, 1976

Part of the land where the South Nahanni River lies had been made into a national park in 1972 by Prime Minister Pierre Trudeau. An ardent canoeist, he had paddled the River previously. When we paddled the River, most of the Park's regulations were not yet in place. In 1978, it was to be the first place named a World Heritage Site by UNESCO (United Nations Education, Scientific and Cultural Organization).

In August 1976, we co-led a fantastic three-week trip on the South Nahanni and the lower Liard rivers in the Northwest Territories. We were blessed with a wonderful group of people. All twelve of us arrived in Watson Lake, Yukon, on scheduled runs. Then, with rented aluminum canoes, we flew in by charter to the Moose Ponds at the headwaters of the River beside the majestic Mount Wilson. Having an elevation of 2,276 metres, it rises like a huge cone that can be seen for vast distances. The mountain sits on the border between the Yukon and the Northwest Territories, dividing the waters that flow to the Mackenzie River and eventually to the Arctic Ocean from the waters that flow to the Yukon River and eventually to the Bering Sea.

For the first six days we descended the "technical" Rock Gardens, a section requiring a high degree of paddling skill, without spray covers. With lots of rocks and lots of swift water to manoeuvre we had several fill-ups and other adventures. In future we would use spray covers in such circumstances.

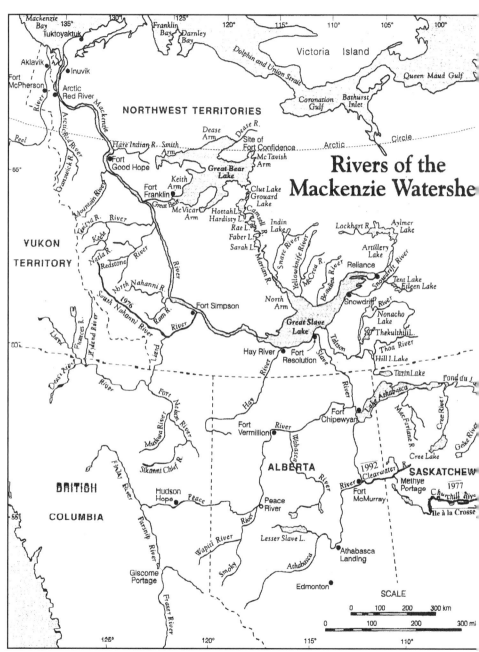

Rivers of the Mackenzie Watershed. *Taken from* Canoeing North into the Unknown, *114*

From our log:

August 11, Day 5:

Up at 7:00; away at 9:30 am, back into the Rock Gardens. Warm, but light showers. We shot many rock-strewn rapids, shipping a good deal of water and thus necessitating bailing or emptying. With low water, however, lining seemed particularly hard. By the mouth of the day's first creek on the right we encountered a beautiful shoal-stone cliff rising straight out of the River. The most complex set involved a great turn to the right in the river followed by a sweep to the left; it lasted over half a mile. Just well into this set, Dick and Dawna Armstrong got broadside to a rock and swamped, with the rock as a fulcrum exactly amidship, and with the inside of the canoe facing upstream. The canoe jammed and started to buckle over the rock as the full current pounded into the ends. Because the Armstrongs happened to be last in the "train," most of us had to walk back along the shore to help. It took 40 minutes and much energy to pry the aluminum canoe loose; just at the moment of release—we used a big pole in the swift current to help pry—the bottom started moving up to the thwarts, and the canoe went into a 90 degree angle. We banged the canoe back into shape after discovering a 2-inch jagged rip. After it was temporarily taped up, Pat Lewtes and Bruce shot it empty through the remaining heavy part of the set, landing on the gravel bar on the left just before the end of the rapids, where the river turned to the left. Opposite, on the right, was a high cliff, and slightly upstream we now noticed the tepee poles from Wanapitei's 1975 campsite. [Marcus Bruce and Mary Ann Haney had led a co-ed "Voyageur" youth trip on the Nahanni the previous year.] It was warm as we spent from 1:00 to 4:30 p.m. repairing the canoe and allowing it to dry. The latter part of the time we had scattered showers and drizzle, so we had to cover the canoe with a tarp. On the move again, we shot some light rapids, one mildly complex set, and then paddled four miles in light current; the valley had opened up. Rain and much cooler. After passing the second clear creek entering on the right and a deep swift, we immediately camped on that side before a set where the river turned hard left under a high, soft rock-shale cliff. Chili dinner which a few people found on the hot side. Trip very wet. Tom Morley caught a 5 lb. Dolly Varden [like a Lake Trout] and two graylings. Bed about 10:00 pm.

We took a day at the mouth of Britnell Creek to hike the thirteen kilometres up to the beautiful Glacier Lake where one can view snow-capped mountain peaks including Mt. Sir James MacBrien (2,062 m.). Further downriver we explored around

Dr. Dick Armstrong on Glacier Lake, viewing Mt. Sir James MacBrien and Mt. Harrison Smith.

Rabbit Kettle Lake, then hiked into the calcium springs. These huge and fascinating tufa mounds of calcium, with a warm pool on top, rise sixty metres (thirty metres high and sixty metres wide). They are the largest such mounds in Canada.

Getting there was difficult, especially fording the Hole-in-the-Wall Creek with its very swift water that came right up to our hips. Carol was swept off her feet and went downstream several hundred metres before reaching the other side. Today, there is a rope to hold onto as one fords the stream.

A few days later, Dominique Guene and Ted Kelly, while paddling too close to shore, suddenly hit a sweeper[2] and flipped over. Despite the very fast current, they were successfully rescued by the Armstrongs (Dick and Dawna) and the La Belles (Jean and Luanne). We spent a day around the breathtaking Virginia Falls, which at one hundred metres is almost twice the height of Horseshoe Falls on the Niagara. At the base we worked on our bright orange tarpaulins to use as makeshift splash covers for use in the four canyons downstream.

From our log:

> Day 15
> … We left at 12:00 noon, into the whitewater of Five Mile Rapids or the Fourth Canyon. This allegedly is the most dangerous section of the trip. We suceeded without taking on more than a cupful of water. Great finesse—we back paddled and ferried to slow our pace. Basically we kept more or less to the left: but everyone must be ready to move to avoid the biggest murky standing waves. It is doubtful that canoes without splash covers could have made it without swamping.
>
> Through the canyon by 12:30, we proceed very quickly down to the top of Figure of Eight Rapids (also known as Hell's Gate), past lots of swifts, some with high waves. Throughout, the scenery—high walls (about 600m.), great vistas, mountain tops, etc. was magnificent… we paddled 24 miles down to

the Gate, Pulpit Rock, a very impressive rock jutting out and up to the height of 46 m., then on past the mouth of the Flat River (the Nahanni's largest tributary) and the Mary River and into the Third Canyon with its 600 m. awesome cliffs and fast current, where the splash covers were helpful. As the rain stopped, we camped at the mouth of end of the Gate on the left at only a fair site… near the mouth of a clear stream in full view of Pulpit Rock itself. Chili and date-orange loaf. Again rain at night.

There was much to admire in the landscape, with the towering craggy rocks, great vistas, and the broad Deadman's Valley as we paddled onward to Nahanni Butte. Another three days were required to paddle the broad Liard River to its junction with the Mackenzie River at Fort Simpson, a small but important Dene community that was once a major Hudson's Bay Post. The Liard River had been in flood from rains in northern British Columbia and the water was still very high. Huge Douglas fir trees had been ripped out "back up there," and were drifting down through the stunted taiga of the lower Liard River. Twice we moored our six canoes to one of these fast-drifting tree trunks, and walked back-and-forth serving and eating lunch.

It was a spectacular trip. One felt very insignificant amidst six-hundred-metre high cliffs, and at other times hemmed in by the dense forest all around. The Nahanni River was very exciting and to some, scary. We enjoyed some fish meals when Tom Morley caught Arctic grayling or Dolly Varden. All around us were traces of wildlife, Dall sheep on the cliffs, many tracks that spoke of bear, both black and grizzly, caribou and moose and sightings of bald eagles—an exceptional natural habitat.

# 12

## THE UPPER CHURCHILL RIVER, SASKATCHEWAN, 1977

As another first for Wanapitei, the upper Churchill River in northern Saskatchewan was our choice for the 1977 two-week adult trip. We canoed east across the central part of the northern part of the province following the old voyageur fur trade highway from the village of Ile-à-la-Crosse on the upper Churchill River. The River in this area is really a series of lakes joined together by fast-moving sections of river. In the 1770s this was an active fur-trading site.[3] We paddled on to the tiny village of Missinipe (below Otter Rapids).

Moving through the parklands, in and out of the Canadian Shield, provided a range of excitement and a range of weather—sunshine, rain and wind. On day three we canoe-sailed for more than sixty kilometres down the latter two-thirds of Lac Ile-à-la-Crosse. Some exciting events of the trip are described in these excerpts from our daily trip log:

> July 16, Day 3:
> Up before 7:00 a.m., away north down the Lake, under a blue sky, and a few "horse" clouds. The southwest tail wind gradually increased its power. We passed Halfway Point, [a large forested promontory] paddling behind the big island, and then amid the islands we came upon rocky points fully white from birds—terns, gulls and pelicans. We lunched on the third island on its lee side. Building a large

sailing rig, with the kitchen tarp and poplar poles, we converted the canoes into a square-rigged catamaran and sailed all afternoon, though at times the wind was rather light.

Finally, we turned into the River, de-rigged, and shot the swifts, which are called Shagwenaw Rapids. Paddling into Shagwenaw Lake we passed the rather large and well-kept Cree village of Patuanak with its new houses, freshly painted and most with large TV antenna; a large relay tower dominates the village and can be seen from Lake Ile. Did not see the point with the great granite outcrop mentioned by Sigurd Olson,[4] so we paddled across the lake and found the River again. We followed its big meanders for several swampy miles, looking for a campsite. Stopping a Chipewayan in an outboard, we learned of a site on the island at the extreme north end of both the 1:50,000 and 1:250,000 maps. We were tired by the time we reached the grassy spot at 9:30 p.m. It was a winter Chipewayan campground recently used for lunches and containing, as was to be common, some rotting fish guts. The site contained a very old but large wooden cross overlooking the River. Dinner of curried rice. Bed late.

July 20, Day 7:

Up at 7:15 a.m. to a clear blue sky and a light west wind. After our fish fry it was hot by the time of our departure at 9:50. We stopped briefly at Elak Dose (which the Indians call Pine River) where four Cree men (their families temporarily at real homes in Patuanak summer here and fish commercially for whitefish and pickerel). Each weekday a Beaver [plane] drops in from Buffalo Narrows; a good daily catch is 800 lbs. of whitefish, which fetches for them 21 cents per lb. but off that comes 13 cents per lb.

for air freight. We paddled into the Churchill River itself and past the mouth of the Haultain River and into the great Haultain Marshes. We stopped at a large granite slope on the right, climbed the ridge and enjoyed a cold lunch amid very hot weather and a beautiful view of the valley. In the afternoon we paddled on down the River, saw our first eagle and took the very narrow northernmost stream, which meanders through the Marsh to the main channel by Dreger Lake. Again saw lots of pelicans. Paddled Dreger and shot the light swifts in the river portion leading into Sandy Lake. Paddled across Sandy to the southeast side, the high Shield side, and camped at 6:50 p.m., on an open sloping face interspersed with spruce and Jack pine. A beautiful view but tent sites a little lumpy. Tired from the heat, we swam to cool down. Dinner of tuna casserole with cookies for dessert. Watched sunset at 9:35 p.m.

July 24, Day 11
Up at 7:10 a.m.; away at 9:10 to a blue sky and some high clouds….About 50 yds before the final turn, on the back side of a small point, we saw a family of campers, our first of the trip. Dropping by for a chat, we shared a poor makeshift lunch spot and soon learned that these Californian [campers] were in some trouble. There were four of them, a middle-aged man, his girlfriend and his two daughters. We heard them loudly calling Igor, Igor…. Missing was the teenaged son who turned up in about an hour. He had the habit of wandering ahead in his canoe, with all the gear and even getting lost; the father was often left with taking the three women in his canoe. Both canoes were cheap, narrow, small, and inadequate fibreglass vessels for a canoe trip. The family had planned a five-day trip on a relatively

easy loop off the La Ronge Road and were already in their eleventh day and running out of food and very depressed. We gave them some of our food, and talked to them about their route... A while after we left and were shooting a set of rapids, we realized Igor had again left the other three and was following us down the set. When he caught up we laid the heavy on him for leaving the rest of the family behind. Soon we came to a campsite where we met up with a Bible group from Regina who were camping there. They said they would look out for the family, as our route was taking a different direction.

Michael Keating preparing his fish for our dinner.

July 25, Day 12:

Al Gamble and Bill McKinley were up early fire lighting. Rest up at 7:00 a.m. Pike chowder cooked by Nicky Lary. Away by 8:50 to a clear sky. We paddled north to the end, of Trout Lake at the voyageur-famous Trout Portage Falls. Carried the gear over the easy 160 yd portage and carefully examined the chute. Mike Keating and Louise Rohanczy decided to run it, despite the very high waves at the base that had to be entered because of a trough on the far right and rocks on the left. Their canoe took about five inches of water in the waves but made it to shore. Carol and Bruce then tried but took on the extra inches of water, filled up and had to swim themselves and the swamped canoe to the left shore; the other two canoes were portaged.

Otter Rapids was a roaring six hundred metres of churning water. The two of us shot first, followed by the others, one canoe at a time. After lunch we paddled out onto Otter Lake and landed at Otter Lake Lodge in the village of Missinipe. We cooked dinner and slept in one of their cabins. The next day the owner drove us south to the Town of La Ronge and on to the city of Prince Albert for our transportation, some by plane, others by bus, back to Ontario. The two of us flew to Sudbury and then drove to Temagami.

What a wonderful collective experience and what an exceptional group of people.

# 13

## THE SPANISH RIVER, 1978

Our trip in 1978 was Wanapitei's first trip on the Spanish River. Our group of fifteen paddled southward, downstream to Agnew Lake Lodge, approximately 150 kilometres from Biscotasing to Agnew Lake Lodge. Today, this is quite a regular route for many diverse groups.

The trip had a rather hectic beginning as recorded in our log:

> Friday, July 14
> Carol, Bruce, Louise [Rohanczy], Pat [Johnson]. Wendy [Cuthbertson] and Jim [Inglis] left Wanapitei about noon in four cars [one with a trailer] with seven canoes and reached Dale St. Clair's home in Chelmsford, north west of Sudbury, at 5:30 where John Clarke (along with Dale) joined us for the drive in two cars [and canoes] north on Highway 144 and on the Ramsay Road to Biscotasing, reaching the village at 9:15. John left with the Hodgins Scout and trailer; [Dale also left].
>
> We camped on an island site about 800 metres from the town, just past the northern gap. Darkness was gathering. Bugs terrible; warm and threatening. Three tents up. Rain hit. At 1:40 am Carol and Bruce paddled into town to meet the CPR's "Canadian" and Ann [Oaks], Gwyneth [Hoyle], Ken [Shonk]

and Dave [Sutton]. At 2:30 paddled "back" in pitch dark as the Bisco lights went out and the sky was deep black. Missed the island by a few metres and wandered about for twenty or so minutes before sorting the world out. More rain later.

Saturday, July 15:
Up at 9:15 to a light drizzle. Back to Bisco at noon to meet the Budd Car [a diesel passenger railcar without a locomotive], and Al [Gamble], Tom [Morley], Marg [Graham] and David [Sutton], but Sheila [Kwiatek, from New York City] not aboard. Air Canada had succeeded in loosing her gear on flight from Toronto. Talked with her on the phone and arranged for her late pick up. Back to campsite and away after lunch about 2:30 [p.m.]. Around the bend and up the long north stretch of the Lake [Biscotasing] against a brisk north wind and some light rain. Stopped at 4:45 at a great site on an island, second of three, one half a mile before the great bend of the Lake. Completed organization of the trip. Good Spirits. Dinner of fresh vegetable stew and chocolate cake. Bed early.

Sunday July 16:
Up at 7:00 am. Sheila arrived by outboard from Bisco. Air Canada had found her gear. She had taken the train north and slept at the station mistress's place. Again met Steve Kelly of Wilderness Seekers and his two adult campers. We had seen him by Bisco with a bitch giving birth to 15 puppies in the bottom of his canoe....

Gwyneth Hoyle's version of the early going of this trip adds some interesting detail:

Saturday, July 15

… The time before the arrival of the next rain was spent organizing the canoes and ropes and tump lines, and deciding the deposition of the various packs.

I chose to stay behind on the tiny island and look after the fire, be ready with the tarpaulin in case of rain, and generally enjoy the peace while the others paddled across to the metropolis of Bisco. They were some time getting back as Sheila's baggage had been left behind by Air Canada and she was still in Sudbury…

First ashore was Tom Morley, gracious English neurosurgeon, who stepped out of the canoe and shook hands. Followed by David Sutton, a small grizzled member of the FON; Al Gamble, very clean-shaven, immaculately correct for the occasion and member of four of Bruce's expeditions; and finally Marg Graham, cheerful, pretty and helpful.

Lunch of grilled cheese sandwiches, almost immediately, then the campsite was packed and the 7 canoes set off… A good campsite appeared just before we turned the corner to run south…

As we started to put up the tents, a beautifully marked black and yellow snake defied us—didn't just hiss, but reared up and struck out in all direction with its forked red tongue. Tom was called to look at it, and while someone held it with a stick, Tom very deliberately put on his tiny gold-rimmed spectacles, took hold of the snake behind the head, opened its mouth and quietly declared the snake brave but harmless, and carried it off to the far end of the island. The tents went up on the spot….[5]

In spite of this unusual start, we had a wonderful trip with high group morale, as shown in the log excerpts that follow:

July 18, Day 5:

Up at 7:30; away at 9:30. After two small swifts we portaged around a 10-foot falls and soon reached the "Big Drop, Double S Curve Rapids," the best of the trip. Wooden canoes and gear were carried over the easy portage on the left. Carol and Bruce shot the sets cutting between big exposed rocks, then centre, right and out by a left exit. Jim Inglis and Pat plus Sheila and Tom followed neatly. Ken Shonk and Wendy Cuthbertson bumped a few times and had a bit of trouble near the bottom. Some canoes were shot twice to give everyone who wanted a try. Louise Rohanczy lost her paddle, with Carol in the bow, and Carol had to finish the set without stern help, as Bruce yelled from the shore, "She'll never make it." That was what alerted her that Louise, in the stern, was without a paddle. Upon hearing that she would never make it, Carol was determined she would get safely to the bottom of the set. They did. Dave made it with Tom. When Jim came down with Gwyneth Hoyle they got slightly off, by the big rocks, filled up, and flipped over. Gwyneth made it to the left shore, and Jim pulled the canoe in to the right, emptied it, and singled the rest of the set.

Soon we were in the long meandering stretch of river running down to the Forks—lunched and rested (fondue and stewed fruit) on a high island campsite by the Forks. About 2½ miles below the Forks, swifts began again; all were shot unscouted. We camped just onto the next map, on the right side, at a sandy beach by a bend in the River. It was a grassy Jack pine grove. Dinner of baked pizza, our own mix. A slow pleasant feast.

The Spanish flows through beautiful, rugged country, sometimes rocky Precambrian, sometimes sandy, especially in the lower reaches. We even found a rare cluster of elm trees that had not been devastated by the Dutch elm disease that had wiped out nearly all of such trees in southern Ontario. As our rather large group gelled, the trip evolved into great fun for all.

# 14

## ON THE COPPERMINE RIVER, NORTHWEST TERRITORIES, 1979

The year 1979 brought another first for Wanapitei. We co-led a trip on the Coppermine River[6] in the Northwest Territories, flying from Yellowknife into Rocknest Lake, then paddling to the Arctic Ocean to what was then called Coppermine and is now Kugluktuk. A relatively large Inuit community right on Coronation Gulf of the Arctic Ocean, it grew significantly in the 1950s when the Inuit were brought in from their more nomadic hunting lifestyle. When we made the trip it was all in the Northwest Territories, but now Kugluktut and most of the section of the Coppermine River, which we paddled are in Nunavut.

The first leg of our journey was from Sudbury to Winnipeg where we had a five-hour layover. We changed planes there and again in Edmonton. Upon arrival in Yellowknife, we discovered that the backpack containing our lifejackets and throw ropes had not arrived. We were not prepared to paddle the Coppermine River without them. Since the mix-up was with Air Canada, Trans Air, which flew us from Edmonton to Yellowknife, felt no responsibility. Our charter from this point was with Wardair, which, with its many bookings, could not change our reservations. Following a lengthy, heated argument with the agent at the air terminal, and wonderful help from Wardair, arrangements were worked out that we would fly due north to our put-in on Rocknest Lake that night. Later, our missing pack would come, at Air Canada's expense, on a special flight.

The first flight (Twin Otter on floats) at 12:15 a.m., carrying Carol

The Rivers of the Western Arctic. *From Canoeing North into the Unknown, 167.*

plus five others, had to fly at a very high altitude due to smoke from ground fires in the area. The flight took 2¼ hours. The second flight, bringing Bruce and the remaining five participants, left Yellowknife at 4:00 a.m. taking 1½ hours, flying very low through light drizzle. Much of the land north of Yellowknife was scrubby, and ill-drained barrens. There was never any real darkness this time of year as the sun set shortly after midnight and rose again within a couple of hours. We spent almost two days at the same campsite, and with some apprehensions we watched many planes fly nearby. Finally, a Beaver Ptarmigan Airline plane landed with our pack, much to our great relief.

The Arctic this time of year was in bloom with its many delicate flowers and flowering small bushes that we had lots of time to admire and photograph. We hiked up behind the campsite to the treeless plateau where we had a panoramic view of the Coppermine River ahead of us and Rocknest Lake behind. We were awed by the landscape. Throughout our trip, especially after we got underway, we saw many birds including tundra "whistling" swans, Arctic terns, bald eagles, northern shrike, rough-legged falcons and gyrfalcons with their young nesting on the banks of high cliffs. We also saw numerous caribou but none in large numbers.

On our second morning en route, a lone canoeist suddenly appeared. He was from Washington, DC, and he had started his journey two weeks earlier at Rae on Great Slave Lake. His plan took him up the Snare River and over the divide to reach the Coppermine River, which he was also following down to the Arctic Ocean.

At some campsites during the evening Bruce would read aloud from photocopies of sections of George Douglas's account of his trip on the lower Coppermine, in his *Lands Forlorn*, published in 1914.[7] George Douglas was, of course, the great adventurer from Lakefield, Ontario, who spent a year paddling and snowshoeing about Great Bear Lake and the Coppermine River

Often we believed that we were camped where Samuel Hearne, John Franklin or George Douglas probably had camped. Along the way were also campsites where Eric and Pamela Morse, Jack Goring, Pierre Trudeau with their group had camped in 1966. (They, of course, were the key members of the second phase of the

Voyageur Club.)   What a depth of feeling for Northern history is represented by such names!

From the log of our trip:

> July 20, Day 9:
>
> Up at 7:30—another day of sunny skies and warm weather. In a morning of fast water, the river was quite narrow. Saw a caribou on the shore in the distance and shortly afterwards as we rounded a bend in the river, we saw another caribou about 50 yards from us. He just looked at us as we paddled by. The current increased. Got to Rocky Defile about 1:00 p.m. Just before these rapids we noted a high gravel hill on the right, which almost looked like a gravel pit pitched on a 45 degree angle; this was followed by a dry boulder fan. We carried our gear across the portage on the right—about ½ mile—very steep, up across a plateau and then a very steep descent down the other side. On top of the hill stood a monument to a young couple, David and Carol Jones, who were drowned in the rapids in August 1972.
>
> Bruce and Carol shot the rapids right of centre but not hard right. They got into position at the beginning and backpaddled and ferried their way through, taking in no more than a cupful of water. Dick Mansfield and Ken Shonk, not backpaddling enough and too far left, got into the large standing waves and swamped. Ken came down holding his cup up offering us a drink of water. He was able to get to shore himself. Dick stayed with the canoe and helped Bruce do a canoe-over-canoe rescue. This was difficult due to the splash covers. During the rescue Carol was able to recover the two paddles and keep the canoe on a good course as it was carried quickly downstream about ½ mile in light rapids. Dick then got his canoe to shore about another ¼ mile further down river where it was left until later.

We then lined the one canoe upstream until opposite the base of the portage and did an upstream ferry across. The others, not being sure that we could get back upstream, portaged the remaining canoes across, in case they were needed. They were disappointed not to shoot, but spirits were high.

We all went for a swim, had a late lunch of cheese fondue with tortillas and corn bread. We started paddling again just before 5:00 p.m., went about 7 miles through light rapids and fast water and arrived at the mouth of the Kendall River at about 6:30 p.m. Did about 20 miles on this day. The upstream bank had on it an Arctic Circle Outpost.

A young couple from Minnesota were preparing for some fishing guests. They fly them in from Hornby Bay (Great Bear Lake). We set up camp on the downstream side of the mouth of the Kendall River. A Cessna arrived at the fishing camp with some gear and soon afterwards a helicopter landed on a gravel island just off the mouth of the Kendall. Five men got out to fish for Arctic char. They soon gave up and departed. In the meantime, Wilf Poley caught a large Arctic char, Bruce lost one, and Tom Morley caught a small grayling. Tom, Sheila Kwiatek and Carol walked a few hundred yards up the Kendall River to where hundreds of swallows had dried mud nests on the limestone cliffs. Dinner at 10:30 p.m. with sun still well above the tree line. Tom was chef in charge of the fish—char steaks with fresh lemon, baked in foil with onions, caraway seed, thyme, and dill. Short rain shower at dinner time—it didn't last long and was followed by a beautiful double rainbow.

On Day 14 we camped about three hundred metres upstream from Bloody Falls where we spent two nights. On the second morning we walked to the base of the rapids where there was a cairn

Sheila Kwiatek and Dr. Tom Morley preparing an Arctic char for dinner. The fish was caught by Dr. Michael Watt.

without a formal plaque. It was to commemorate the massacre, hence the name "Bloody Falls," as witnessed by Samuel Hearne in 1771, when a total Inuit encampment, men, women and children, were slain by the Chipewyan who were escorting Hearne from the Hudson Bay and the Churchill River to Coronation Gulf.

Later in the day we hiked up a high hill behind our campsite to a flat plateau—the walking was good—where we had a tremendous view and our first view of the Arctic Ocean some twenty kilometres downstream. On our return we picked up a large caribou antler and on the high cliff just above the falls, Ken discovered a large bald eagle's nest with one young in it. Once back, three of our members, Janine Poley, Ken and Carol, went swimming in a quiet deep pool near the lower end of portage.

Following dinner of rice, vegetables, cheese and nutballs, we had a visitor. Ingmar Remmler (he was camping below the Falls with a group) arrived with two freshly caught inconnue (a species of large Arctic fish) all ready to cook. We baked them and had a delicious bedtime lunch.

The next day we paddled two-and-a-half hours out onto Coronation Gulf of the Arctic Ocean and along the shore to the nearby village of Coppermine (now Kugluktuk), where we spent several hours exploring before our flight out of the area.

# PART THREE:

# FROM NORTHERN ONTARIO
# TO THE FAR NORTH, 1980–1989

# 15

## THE LADY EVELYN AND MAKOBE RIVERS, 1980

In 1980 we went on a great circular Temagami area route with our group, calling it the "Trout Streams Special." We flew, however, into Florence Lake (so named by the geological surveyor of the time), high up the Lady Evelyn system from Camp Wanapitei. From Florence, we descended the North Branch of the Lady Evelyn, then the Seven Sisters, a series of small, narrow, shallow rapids, usually shootable only in June or early July, of the main river.

Our route then took us up the tiny Grays River, and we crossed Gray Mud Lake with difficulty. The muck in that lake was almost up to the surface, with the actual bottom somewhere below the length of our paddles. Standing in our canoes, we pushed with great effort against the slimy muck; each canoe was completely on its own. From one of the participants came a sound that signalled something close to panic. She cried out that we should get a plane or helicopter to rescue us, otherwise we were facing certain doom. But even today this would be out of range of all cellphones and a world with satellite phones did not yet exist. As we kept talking to her, telling her to calm down and to stand up and push harder with her paddle through the muck, we were slowly making our way through.

We portaged over the small divide from the Grays River to the Makobe River, down its light whitewater and into Elk Lake. From there we paddled down the Montreal River past Mountain Chutes (which we shot a few times for fun), portaging west to Mendelson Lake and down the creek-pond system to the small Anvil Lake, just northeast of Maple Mountain. Here, while we set up camp, Tom Morley unearthed an authentic aboriginal arrowhead, which he took home and had its authenticity verified at the Royal Ontario Museum. Once the campsite was in place, we continued on to Tupper Lake, climbed Maple Mountain, then returned to Anvil for the night.

The next morning we portaged into Sucker Gut and paddled on to Lady Evelyn and Diamond lakes to Lake Temagami, and eventually reached home base. Beautiful weather and scenery helped establish and maintain a very positive group morale throughout our time together. The participants were: Al Gamble, Gwyneth Hoyle, Bill McKinley, Dr. Tom Morley, Patricia Pell, Janine and Wilf Poley and Dr. Ken Shonk, all of whom (except for Pat Pell) had paddled with us before.

The following two paragraphs are an updated version of a report written for trippers in the mid-1970s, by Bruce Hodgins and Tom Roach, Wanapitei's assistant director from 1974–78.

> Many experts regard the Lady Evelyn as the most beautiful river valley in all of Northeastern Ontario. What geographers call an immature stream, the River

Bill McKinley and others lining the rapids on the Makobe River.

rises in a multitude of high-elevation, headwater swamps. It is headwaters country. The River flows together from various little branches and tributaries and cascades down over a multitude of shallow rapids and complex falls. The Lady Evelyn, the centre of a Provincial Park, is part of the large Montreal River Basin, the most northerly one in Ontario that flows into the Ottawa at Lake Temiskaming.

After the North Branch, the South Branch and the Florence River of the Lady Evelyn system join at the Forks, the combined River travels over many little rapids, (the Seven Sisters) before entering Macpherson Lake, where it picks up the water of the Grays River. Then, after a complex falls (locally called Shangri-la) and two more rapids, it enters Katherine or Divide Lake where it redivides, into the North Channel and the South Channel. Before each portion reaches Lady Evelyn Lake, it passes over several more falls, on the South Channel over Twin Falls, Bridal Veil and the one at Fat Man's Squeeze. On the North Channel, the water flows over Helen's, Centre and Frank's Falls. All these falls are more than six metres high. Downstream, the River passes relatively close to the base of Maple Mountain, the second highest spot in Ontario.

The upper Lady Evelyn River exhibits the typical headwater features of a small river. Plant communities vary according to the dryness of the soil. Small eskers and old river banks harbour stands of jack, red and white pine, while the wetter intervals and swamps support black spruce and older communities. Ducks are a common feature of this part of the trip. It should be noted that the original name for this waterway was the "Majamaygos" or Trout Streams. The area was a favourite summer hunting and trapping ground for local Temagami First Nation, especially the Katt family,[1] due to the abundance of speckled trout, ducks, beaver and moose and, in earlier times, woodland caribou and deer.[2]

The eighties were just beginning for these two paddling partners; there would be return trips to the Lady Evelyn.

# 16
## ON TO THE THELON, 1981

Our 1981 canoe trip on the Thelon River[3] was our third in the Northwest Territories, and took us into the area now part of Nunavut. Our group was flown into the Hanbury-Upper Thelon confluence from Yellowknife. For two weeks we explored and paddled our way down the Thelon, to the point where we were picked up, the stretch between Beverley Lake and the huge Aberdeen Lake, and then flown east to Baker Lake, which is, of course, now in Nunavut. Baker Lake is the only inland Inuit community, and, strange as it may seem, it is at the geographic centre of Canada.

En route, we visited the "Warden's Grove," and examined the grave sites of the starved (in the winter of 1926–27) John Hornby, his eighteen-year-old cousin, Edgar Christian, and Harold Adlard. All was recorded in our log:

> Tuesday July 14:
> Up at 6:45, away at 8:30. Weather warm, but a light headwind. Reached the Hornby cabin site in just over an hour. The big white stone is the indicator, but the ruins are in-shore 75 metres, and about 50 metres downstream from the rock. From one small spot on the River the three crosses on the graves are visible. The cabin used by the three starvation victims in 1926–27 is in very bad condition; only parts of the walls survive.

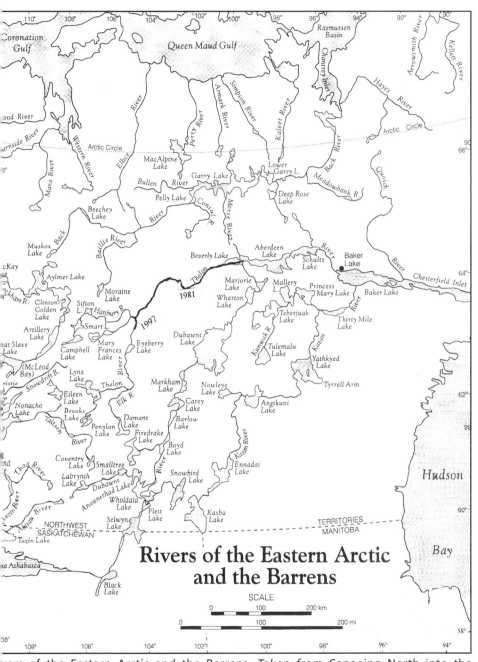

Rivers of the Eastern Arctic and the Barrens. *Taken from* Canoeing North into the
Unknown, 100.

In the spring before the trip, Bruce was reading George Whalley's *Death in the Barrenlands*[4] concerning the death of the three men. At the time Bruce had at home a copy from the Trent University library of David Hanbury's *Sport and Travel in the Northland of Canada* published in 1904.[5] Hanbury was a British adventurer who spent three years in the Canadian North, 1901–03, travelling by canoe and snowshoe, mainly in the Hanbury-Thelon watershed but also on parts of the Lockhart, Back and Armiack rivers. The Hanbury River was named for him in the early part of the twentieth century. Reading Whalley's book on Hornby's death, Bruce discovered that Hornby had visited with George Douglas (the expert on the Coppermine River) in his Lakefield, Ontario, home, just before Hornby set out on his fatal trip. Bruce learned from *Death in the Barrenlands* that Hornby had read Douglas' copy of *Sport and Travel* while on his visit to Lakefield. The widow of George Douglas had recently given her husband's library to Trent. Bruce suddenly realized that the copy of Hanbury's book that he had just read and was lying beside him, was the very copy that Hornby had been reading before he set out on that fatal trip. What an eerie feeling!

The grave markers of John Hornby, his young cousin, Edgar Christian, and Harold Adlard. The three of them starved to death in the early spring of 1927.

This northern trip was a big influence on Bruce and on Gwyneth Hoyle (a participant on the trip) and they soon began researching for the book *Canoeing North Into the Unknown: A Record of Travel, 1874 to 1974*. Both were so very interested in the history of travel on the north-flowing rivers of the country, that their research would consume much of the next three years of their lives.

Thursday, July 16, Day 7:
Up at 6:45 a.m. Elliot Rodger caught two large lake trout (he caught by far, the most fish). Away at 8:30. Hot and buggy! We paddled down to a spot opposite Muskox Hill, which cannot be seen from the River or shore. All but the Patersons (Bill and Diane) and Ian Dagg walked the six kms to the pingo [an ice-cored hill pushed up from the permafrost], which is Muskox Hill. This pingo is unique to the Western Arctic; pingos are common to the lower Mackenzie. It looked like a huge sand castle or ancient Celtic ruin, turrets on top, rising out of the tundra plain. In the distance we saw, at last, a muskox half way up Muskox Hill. He descended the hill, moving to the lake on the left (west side). We circled to see him up close. Theo [Hoffman], and especially Carol, got to within a few yards of the huge beast—excellent photos. Then we climbed the pingo, which is surrounded by a natural swamp moat. It is above the bug line and thus a delight for all of us.

After walking back, we had a cold lunch and pushed off at 2:00 p.m. Almost immediately we saw another muskox, close up on the left bank. We suddenly became aware, however, of a storm approaching from the rear with large black clouds and bugs, unbelievably bad, even out on the River itself. No relief. We pulled out on the left bank by the tiny creek in the marshy section where the Thelon flows due south. The storm hit, hard for only four minutes. Beyond the narrow marge was only bare

Gwyneth Hoyle and Theo Hoffman coming back to the campsite with a load of driftwood for the cooking fire.

tundra for miles. Light rain continued, so we set up the tents and cooked dinner. Rain stopped.

Elliot [Rodger] with great exertion and help, caught the largest trout of the trip. Then he lost another. Bill Paterson also got a big one. The fish were leaping all over the place in the post-storm stillness. We had dinner of fish from the morning's catch, plus a stew of vegetables and dumplings. Very high morale, mellow evening—though the bugs soon returned. Large muskox tracks on the beach.

Friday, July 17:
Up at 6:45, away at 8:50. Wind out of the north increasing. We paddled on to the cabin of the Canadian Wildlife service jut before Lookout Point. It is located downstream from a bear-proof cache site with an old red stern Rupert canoe stashed in small trees. We met a three person federal research team led by Don Thomas and Hank Killoon. They served us coffee. Their project focused on the effect of insects on caribou migration patterns.

Downstream a half km we came to a new cabin and some tents. This is exactly at Lookout Point opposite the mouth of the Finnie River and is the location of another research team made up of Frank Moore of the Federal service and three Territorial researchers. They are studying the caribou herd, the number which they had estimated from a plane a few days earlier. It numbers about 93,000 down from the 200,000 ten years earlier.

Monday, July 20:
Up at 7:15, away at 9:15, warm with a clear sky. Shot some swifts and paddled through the Thelon Bluffs. We shot some swifts close to the right side to avoid the large waves on the left.. We then climbed the Bluffs on the higher left side to a small summit where we found the usual small rock pile. We had a great panoramic view, not seen from down on the river… We saw two caribou on the right, then a muskox… a total of eight.

Wednesday, July 22:
Windbound. Up at 6:45, noting no wind abatement at all. Immobilized. Attempted again to use the radio no luck [later found out we had been given the wrong frequency]. A morning of reading, bridge playing, foraging for driftwood and baking. Saw two sandhill cranes. Lunch. Only a very slight wind abatement. Long discussions about the situation. Various viewpoints temperately expressed. Decided on a long walk to the northeast end of the island to check out the north wind which we would have to face in 6 km. Saw a caribou on the beach across on the mainland. Watched some tiny Lapland longspurs…to bed early and up at 3:30 a.m. [The wind is usually less in the early morning.] We had

to make up time in order to catch an arranged flight from Aberdeen Lake to the village of Baker Lake.

Two members of our group, Ann Dagg and Ann Oaks, were both biologists. Ann D. was most interested in wild animal scatology, while Ann O. knew so much about the plants and flowers. Theo also was very knowledgeable about the flowers and, as well, was an avid and expert birdwatcher. We still have the list he sent to us of the twenty-six flowers he identified and the forty-seven species of birds.

We were well supplied with fish as Lynn McDonald and Gwyneth did some fishing, and Meredith Rodger sometimes paddled so Elliot could troll for fish. Meredith and Diana also spent a lot of time helping with meal preparation and clean-up—their efforts always much appreciated.

This trip on the Barrens opened our eyes to a new part of the country, realizing the vast differences in topography within the area, the many animals, the delicate and numerous tiny flowers that bloom, and the vast wide open areas where one can turn around while getting a 360-degree view. Theo Hoffman listed over thirty plants and about forty-two birds. It is considered wilderness by many, but one must realize to the Inuit it is homeland.

# 17

## DOWN THE TEMAGAMI AND THE FRENCH RIVERS AND ON TO KILLARNEY, 1982

Our trip in the summer of 1982 took us from Lake Temagami down the Temagami River, in ultra low water, onto a section of the lower Sturgeon River. A short "portage" truck haul carried us to Cache Bay on Lake Nipissing. From there we paddled across the "corner" of the large lake, by Sandy Island, and down the full length of the French River and its Voyageur's Channel, also in ultra low water. Our route led us out onto Georgian Bay, west past Point Grondine and through Collins Inlet, and on to Killarney village.

Our very large group included: Bob Gamble, Shelagh Grant, Barb and Daryl Hodgins, Norman Ito, Pat Johnson, Maryke Kamphuys, Bill McKinley, Lynn McDonald, Tom Morley, Mel Shakespeare, Dale Standen, Bill and Diana Paterson. The following excerpt from the daily log highlights the nature of the trip.

> July 25, Day 11:
> Up at 6:00 and away at 7:45 against a very light wind with a clearing sky. The entrance to the French River's Voyageur Channel entrance was dry! We had to lift over about one yard of shallows and then 10 yards totally dry. After a pond we came to a five-foot-wide "rapid" flowing upstream from Georgian Bay into the pond…so the Bay was now higher than this cut-off part of the Channel. Just before noon we stopped on a beautiful pine-topped granite island

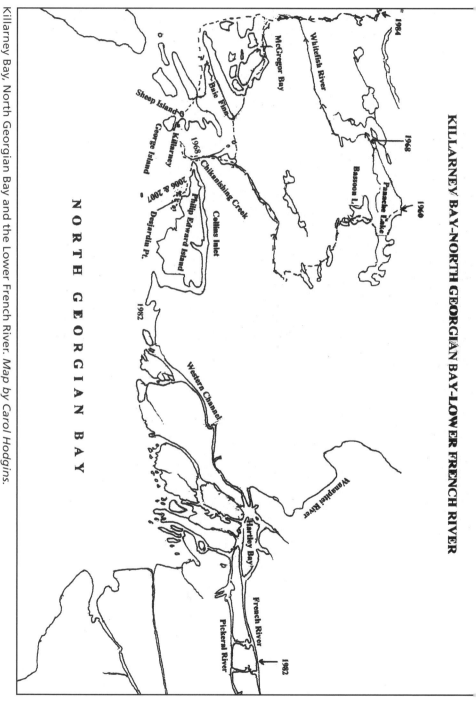

Killarney Bay, North Georgian Bay and the Lower French River. *Map by Carol Hodgins.*

which served our many needs… Its top ridge gave us a view of the open Georgian Bay. Its trees sheltered us from the heat, with its clean sculptured rock sloping into the water.

At 2:30 we left our island, but after about one mile we were forced ashore by big waves and heavy headwind. We camped there (by the Sudbury-Manitoulin District Boundary) on an open site, which had many flat rocky expanses and which was large enough for dozens of tents. Before and after our dinner of chilli and nutballs, much time was spent with our faces upwind smelling the moist lake air and gazing at the Grondine Light and the great elusive Point Grondine some five miles across the open, shoal-strewn Bay. At 7:30 p.m., with the wind still high, we decided to pitch the tents and try for an early start in the a.m.

That evening, Carol met a "friendly," rather large rattlesnake while wandering around the area; it was viewed by many and well-photographed. Daryl Hodgins' assertion, "there are no rattlesnakes north

We hiked to the top of Leading Mark Hill near Killarney (Georgian Bay).

of the French" had to be revised to exclude the ripararian's first 100 metres. Bed at 9:30.

We paddled through Collins Inlet and into the harbour of the village of Killarney—all on the Voyageur Highway to the Northwest. Our last night was at the cottage of Daryl and Barbara Hodgins in Killarney Bay. Except for the brief "truck portage," we had paddled all the way from Lake Temagami, down the full Temagami and French rivers to Georgian Bay and the village of Killarney, on such a great historic route. That route was all in the Canadian Shield, but the changing scenes were spectacular. Some sections seem remote, while others sections are populated, but the various communities are very different. Happily, the French River is now protected both as a Provincial Park and as a designated Heritage River.

# 18
## THE BELL-PORCUPINE AND TAKHINI RIVERS OF THE YUKON, 1983

The Bell-Porcupine trip was in the far northern part of the Yukon Territory in sight of the Northwest Territories border. We flew into Summit Lake by the Richardson Pass. From there, we proceeded down the Little Bell, the Bell and the Porcupine rivers to the Gwitchin (Dene) village of Old Crow. This community located on the Porcupine River at the mouth of the small Old Crow River, is the only one in the Yukon that is north of the Arctic Circle.

We had planned on paddling until the Porcupine flows into the Yukon River at Fort Yukon, Alaska, but a pre-trip finger injury sustained by Shelagh Grant became infected so plans changed, and we flew out from Old Crow.

This particular trip demonstrates the complications that sometimes can arise when meeting up with a group. We met Bill and Diana Paterson and Ken Shonk at the airport in Toronto. Doreen and Myk Bartlett joined us at the Vancouver airport and from there we soon flew to Whitehorse. Here the Patersons left us, flying to Inuvik to see the town before the canoeing began. Shelagh and Jon Grant and Lynn McDonald also flew to Inuvik. We were then all to meet up at Fort Macpherson. However, due to weather, the plane with Shelagh, Jon and Lynn McDonald went directly to Summit Lake.

Lois Pope, (a former Trent student of Bruce's, living outside Whitehorse) was to drive the five of us from Whitehorse to Fort McPherson, after going to Watson Lake to pick up the Wanapitei Suburban. It had been driven west earlier, part of a Voyageur II

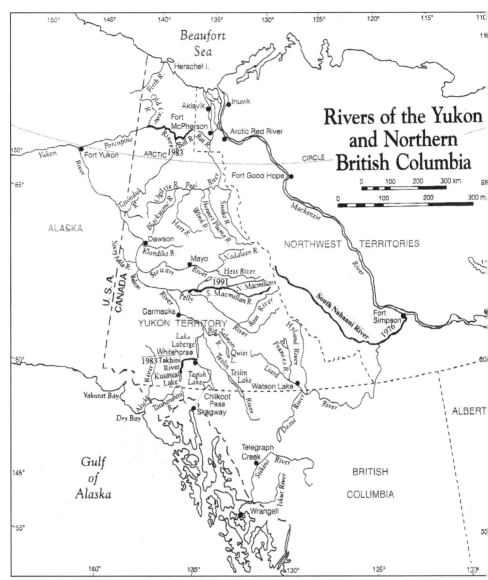

Rivers of the Yukon and Northern British Columbia. *Taken from* Canoeing North into th
Unknown, *186.*

co-ed trip from Camp Wanapitei in Temagami. They were to hike
the Chilkoot Pass and then paddle the Little and South Nahanni.
(This trip was led by Hilary Heath and our son Shawn Hodgins.)
Lois also picked up six canoes that Wanapitei had previously stored
in Watson Lake. She was still nursing six-week-old Caitlin, who was

with her. Jacques Lacost, a friend of Lois's, followed behind the Suburban in his pick-up truck as we did not want Lois to be alone with a tiny baby, should she have any van problems.

Leaving Whitehorse about 6:00 p.m. (Yukon time), we stopped for a few supplies and headed north on the Klondike Highway. At 10:00 p.m. we arrived at Pelly Crossing, which is close to where the Pelly River enters the Yukon River and near the abandoned HBC's Fort Selkirk. It is also where the bridge on the Whitehorse to Dawson City Highway crosses the Pelly River.

The next morning we discovered problems with the wheel bearings on the great green trailer, and Jacques had a flat. We stopped for repairs at an Esso Station at the Dempster Highway turn off. It took until 4:00 p.m. to fix the van for as well as the bearings, it needed a new U-joint.

Here, by prior arrangement, we picked up two more of our canoeing group, Meredith and Elliot Rodger from Ottawa. Finally, we were on our way with seven of our tripping group. We enjoyed the gorgeous mountain views and colourful tundra beside the rivers we passed. That night we camped at an official site by Engineer Creek, a tributary of the large Ogilvie River. We met up with Bill and Diana Paterson in Fort McPherson and from there flew into Summit Lake where we met up with the others.

The Grants flew directly home. The others flew to Dawson City where Lynn parted company with us. The remaining nine of us then flew back to Whitehorse, and drove north, up the Takhini Valley and paddled the Takhini River downstream to the Alaska Highway.

> Suburban trip, August 7:
> We lunched along the shores of the Klondike River. The scenery was gorgeous around Tombstone Mountain and by the divide between the Klondike and the Blackstone rivers. Colourful tundra along the upper reaches of the Blackstone....

> August 8:
> Road changed repeatedly in quality—some bits only fair, others smoother with a black shale-like surface.

At Summit Lake in the Yukon, the great watershed divide. McDougall Pass is in the background.

Passed only four big trucks. Glorious scenery as the road follows directly beside the mighty Ogilvie [River], which looked very paddleable with many good gravel rapids. The scenery even improved going up and over the pass onto the Eagle Plains, with the Ogilvie Mountains to the right. Saw a long tailed jaeger….

August 9:
The first thing we did in Fort McPherson, NWT was to check in with the RCMP [something one always does before heading into the far north for any canoe trip]. We also phoned Aklak Air in Inuvik to co-ordinate our flights. Then we visited the grave sites of the Lost Patrol[6] and the new Community Centre, which had recently been officially opened by Trudeau. We then drove to the dock area to find our charter plane….

The first flight from Inuvik and across the divide, back into the Yukon, to Summit Lake was at 9:00 p.m., with the Patersons, Grants and Lynn McDonald. The flight had been held up several hours due to winds. They flew directly over the Mackenzie Delta. The Beaver then flew to Fort McPherson for those of us who had driven there by van, along with the canoes and the gear. It was 3:30 a.m. when our third flight landed at Summit Lake in the Yukon. The sun was down, but there was no real night at 67° N and we had had fantastic views flying up the Rat River Valley from the flatlands of the Peel-Mackenzie Delta. As we flew through the Richardson Pass it felt as if one could touch the mountains on either side of the plane (if only one could reach out with one's arms). The locals call Summit Lake both Loon and Caribou.

The following excerpts from the trip log provide some of the highlights of our trip:

> August 10, Day 1: Summit Lake
> Up leisurely at 9:00 a.m. or so, to a fantastic sight, clear sky, calm little lake surrounded by mountains and valleys stretching in various directions. Our site was a mossy peninsula at the southwest side of the lake. We washed clothes and swam in the cool 50°F water. The outlet creek was explored. After a cold lunch, we hiked up the mountains behind our site, looked into the full valley of the Little Bell and west toward the Bell River itself. Myk [Bartlett] and Doreen, and Ken [Shonk] went right up to the peak, with Carol and Lynn [Mcdonald] stopping on the right just short of it.
>
> Back at the site, two Germans arrived before dinner, very tired after a 15-day haul up the Rat River with their canoe. Low water. We (guests included) feasted on huge Alberta steaks brought in by Jon and Shelagh. We also had salads etc. Magnificent evening. Some bugs until the temperature fell. [Perhaps the best evening of the entire trip—BWH.] Three of

us checked out a cross-tundra route of about 500 metres directly from the west side of the Lake to the Little Bell, avoiding the clogged exit creek. It did have a steep bank to descend down to our put-in, on the stream, which was about seven metres wide. Others fished.

August 13, Day 4:

...Arrived at La Pierre House at 12:30. Though invisible from the river, the ruins of the long abandoned [1911] HBC Post was easy to locate, from careful use of the topographical maps. The remains are up a high bank and back about 50 metres. They include three buildings, plus older ruins. We lunched on the flats, with cold nut loaf. More and more trees in the area. Shoreline heavily covered with grizzly and moose tracks, but we only saw lots of geese, Arctic loons and osprey....

Diana Paterson, Bruce and Carol in front of the abandoned HBC Post, La Pierre House.

August 14, Day 5:

...We lunched in clear sight of impressive and forested Mason Hill to our west; it had an apparent man made "rim," along one side, that we were told was an old abandoned airstrip. We reached the Porcupine River, coming in on our left, at 4:10 p.m.; it was very wide but no faster than the Bell—rather disappointing to us, with unfortunate consequences yet to be determined. We immediately swung northward, thus passing west of prominent Mason Hill. We camped at 6:00, again on the left, on the latter part of the major curve about 12 km. down from the confluence. Hot rum toddies appreciated. Chili dinner of beans, bulgur salad with locally picked mint and chives. A large family of Old Crow Indians (the Bruces and Benjamins) visited us from their flat, big bowed, planked outboard. They remarked on the unusual low water. They were out looking for moose....However, with the extra slow current, we were not at all keeping up with the hard pace set by Eric Morse's group in 1965. We decided, nevertheless, to try and reach Old Crow by Tuesday night; we had 86 miles [140 km] to go in two days....

August 16, Day 7:

Up river from the village we stopped at Ken Nukan's camp on the riverbank on the right. Ken is a traditionalist Indian (Loucheux) living most of the time along with his huskies at this site, though his grandson Gerald, and often visitors, especially German canoeists and kayakers, stay with him. We learned a lot from old Ken. He though the caribou would cross in three or four days...[Shelagh and Jon Grant flew out from Old Crow the next day].

August 18, Day 9:

The village of Old Crow is on the Porcupine River just below the mouth of the Old Crow River. Our campsite for four nights was on a point at the downstream end of a sandy island, about a 200 metre paddle from the village, where we spent most of our time for three days. We interacted with so many of the local people, both Loucheux and Euro/Canadian and American. The first thing was to check in with the Chief, Johnny Abel. We also met Randal Charlie who was village and band manager. We met RCMP Corporal Dave Henderson and his wife Kunie, later spending time with them. We took about a 12-mile hike up the east foothills of Old Crow Mountain but did not see any caribou.

Some of us had tea with the Anglican Rev. Brown, a delightful but rather sad, ageless man—a Winnipeg medieval history scholar of the spread of the Eastern Church in Byzantine times, long before

Low water at the bank of the Porcupine River by Old Crow. In high water the level is up to the top of the bank.

the spread of Islam. He had taken Canadian history from the late W.L. Morton who became Chancellor at Trent [and was himself a canoeist]. In the evening we were invited to attend an Anglican christening where most of the singing was in Loucheux. The Bishop of the Yukon had flown in, piloting his own Cessna, to conduct the service.

August 19, Day 10:
…Then we went to the softball tournament, Canadian Loucheux championships involving Old Crow, Aklavik and Fort McPherson …Twin Otters were flying in male and female teams, but first there was a warm-up game between Old Crow "As" and "Bs." The "Bs" team was short a player, so Ken [Shonk] played outfield for them…. Diana and Bill [Paterson] joined us after they had a lavish dinner with two locals, Abraham and Mary Peter, which featured huge caribou steaks and wild cranberries. While Old Crow and Aklavik males and Ken met in a pre-tournament match, the Bartletts and Hodgins retired with Chief Able (his wife Rosalie was with us part of the time) to his mother's home for tea and much talk. We learned so much about Old Crow…Doreen [Bartlett] had to fend off the many young admirers of her reddish hair, much to general amusement of all.

August 20, Day 11:
We had met Karen [Rinker], and today met her husband, Roger Rinker; they staffed the Evangelical Mission. Roger had just returned from Fairbanks [Alaska] having taken an airplane mechanics course.

We were able to arrange flights with Roger in the Mission's Cessna to fly over the area where we might see the caribou. Those on the 1½ hour first flight saw about 100 caribou and a grizzly bear. Those on the next flights saw about 1,000 caribou. The plane flew north of Old Crow and west downstream towards the Alaska border. Soon after the flights our DC3 Charter was ready to fly out the ten of us, six canoes and all our gear. The pilot was John Peacock, the stewardess, his wife Marion, plus a co-pilot. The two hour flight to Dawson City was magnificent with John pointing out all the sights. We did the usual things in [that city Dawson], saw Robert Services's cabin—dined, took in the Gas Light Follies, and ended up at Diamond Tooth Gertie's.

August 21, Day 12:
This morning, Lynn [McDonald] departed so now we were nine. We took the tour to the Bonanza gold diggings, and Dredge No.4. Then we took our flight to Whitehorse where we did some more sightseeing.

August 22, Day 13:
We drove up the Alaska Highway about 40 miles [64 km], then southward on a twisty dirt road to the long narrow Kusawa Lake, stretching toward Kluane and the BC border, with many glacier topped mountains. We put into Kusawa Lake after lunch. Riding a fairly strong tailwind we quickly left this beautiful Lake behind and entered the Takhini River itself. Right away we were into heavy swifts and class one or more rapids. The River was wider than the Bell, but narrower and deeper than the Porcupine. We paddled the next couple of days and were picked up on August 24th at the bridge where the Alaska Hwy crosses the River.

We had a wonderful time paddling on the Takhini River, a place we had not planned to be.

It had been a wonderful if rather strange trip. We saw the scenic Yukon in its very remote reaches on the Porcupine River, in Old Crow, Whitehorse and Dawson (almost rebuilt as a living historic site). Even the drive on the Dempster Highway was spectacular. Then there was the short but splendid run on the Takhini River. Fantastic memories.

# 19

## ON THE UPPER WANAPITEI RIVER, THE SPANISH RIVER AND ON TO KILLARNEY, 1984

We drove from Wanapitei on the bush road route north and west to the upper Wanapitei River and then paddled its entire descent to Lake Wanapitei in 1984. We then crossed the Lake to a road landing in its northwest angle. The water level was exceedingly high, and the River continued to rise under very heavy rains for the next four days. A couple of portages and low areas were totally awash. In some places we had to walk with our gear, in water almost up to our hips. The River was very challenging and great care was required to make our way long its length. Many in the group had previously not known each other, and morale was often hard to sustain with the persistent rain and tougher going.

When we came to the crossing of a very old lumber road, one couple decided they were going to leave the trip. At that point, we were many miles north of Sudbury. It took us about an hour trying to convince them to stay. When they understood the fact that they would have a very long walk and that it would be their responsibility to get the canoe back to the Camp, they somewhat reluctantly decided to continue with us. Fortunately, the weather took a change for the better, and with the sun out and the comfort of being warm and dry, morale went away up. The rest of the trip was much more fun.

We had an interesting young Greek-Canadian couple with us. He was a musician who had spent two years playing in the band on "The Love Boat" in the Caribbean, and had lots of stories to share. Some months later we went to the couple's wedding at The Old Mill in Toronto.

In August of that year we rallied in Sudbury with many of our more regular participants. Most of us driving Highway 144 and the bush route north to Biscotasing. For a week we paddled the Spanish River to Agnew Lake in very high water. From Agnew Lake we were picked up, in the wee hours of the morning, by the Camp minibus, which was six hours late, after having been used to put-in a lower Dumoine River trip.

We were transported south of Espanola to Birch Island and a back channel of McGregor Bay on Georgian Bay. From there we canoed through the sheltered maze of islands, channels and points, crossing short portages and ultimately arriving at the Killarney Bay cottage of Barbara and Daryl Hodgins, vital members of our trip group. Others included Shelagh and Jon Grant, Dick Mansfield, Laurie Morrison, Heather and Gerry Quengesser, Bill, Alex and David Taylor and Charles Vogl.

From our daily log comes some highlights of the trip:

> August 12, Day 2:
> Up at about 7:00 a.m. to a breakfast already being prepared by Jon and Shelagh Grant (which was happily always their pattern). Away by 9:30 to the outlet dams. We carried the gear and canoes over the short carry just left of the right-hand or minor dam and out onto the West Branch. We reached the falls for a lunch on what was in this high water an island between two channels of the falls. We carried over the gear. Carol and Bruce shot the main or right-hand channel in the left V, through three big curlers, and took in considerable water. The

Grants came next, followed by Charles Vogl and David Taylor. Dick Mansfield and Laurie Morrison flipped with the Femat, but the rescue was simple. Bruce then shot safely, first with Alex Taylor, then with Laurie, and then alone. Nearly all of us had a relaxing swim before lunch under clear skies and warm temperatures. Daryl Hodgins caught a very good-sized pike.

Leaving at 2:20, we paddled 2 km. to the top of the complex of four rapids. The water seemed too high and turbulent to cope with more than short sections of the complex, so we portaged the whole series along a good trail running for 600 m. on the right. At the base, while a few swam, Daryl hooked a "huge" pickerel, but it got away when it was right up to the shore. We paddled on for close to 2 km., shot a short set on the left and then, after another 2 km., came to the small gorge-like approach to the second falls, portaging on the left. Bruce singled the complex lower rapids portion of the run, followed

Shooting whitewater on the Spanish River.

by Shelagh and Jon. (In July 1978, with lower water, this is where we had practised whitewater runs). After some confusion at this portage (we almost decided to camp at the picturesque but buggy site halfway across the carry) we proceeded about 7 km. to a campsite on the left, at a rocky point where the River opened out with a significant widening.

Following Daryl's pike as hors d'oeuvres, we feasted on blé au gratin and oatmeal cookies with blueberries. Beautiful full moon, orange on rising.

We were transported past Espanola to Birch Island and a back channel of McGregor Bay on Georgian Bay. For three days we canoed east through the sheltered maze of islands, channels and points, crossing short portages and ultimately arriving at the Killarney Bay cottage of Barbara and Daryl Hodgins.

This was a wonderful and almost perfect trip except for some heavy rain during the last two days. The experience even prompted Richard Mansfield to write a poem "The Spanish River Saga," extolling the features of the trip.[7]

# 20

## THE BAZIN IN QUEBEC AND THE MAGNETAWAN IN ONTARIO, 1985

We were flown north into Parent in northern Quebec by bush plane from Ste. Anne-du-Lac, itself north of Mont Laurier, the meeting point for this year's group. Nearby, we put into the Bazin River, and paddled its full length amid great whitewater, at very high levels and running very fast. Some of the rapids were very challenging. Often there were no portages and, if there were at other times, they were barely discernible. Care was certainly required. Sometimes we were walking in the water, lining down the canoes, scrambling over and between rocks.

Daryl Hodgins, Shelagh Grant, Don and Lynda Mason were all experienced whitewater paddlers who had been with us many times before. Joanne Culley and Mike McMurtry had some experience in rapids, but the steady pace of the river was a bit much for them. When hitting one rock, they were not able to slide around it and were not quick enough in exiting the canoe before it broached. The canoe filled up with water and took quite a beating. It took some time to get everything dried out and the "sick-looking" canoe repaired so that we could carry on.

None of us had met Charles Conway from Montreal, before. He was a novice in white water but a very fast learner. Ann Oaks, a biology professor at McMaster, had been with us on the rather calm flat water trip on the Thelon River, where she was interested in seeing the tundra with its birds, animals and flowers. It was a surprise to see her on this trip with so many rapids. She and Charles had some adventures coming down the river, but the canoe always reached the bottom in the upright position. At the end of the trip in her very deep voice, she said, "Carol, some people are lake-water people and some people are river-water people. I think that I am a lake person and you are a river person."

Daryl and Shelagh had agreed to paddle together, but Daryl had jokingly stated to Shelagh, "No matter what difficulties we might have, it will definitely be your fault." In the last rapids they had a classic broach. Like most of us they had minor scrapes from rocks during the long paddle, but when they broached on the rock they claimed to the group that it was the "moccasin monster" that finally got them! Afterwards, Daryl did admit, quietly, that it had been his error. It took several people about half an hour to free the damaged canoe.

The boreal spruce forest usually ran down close to the shoreline. The Bazin campsites were usually very narrow and covered with small scrub second growth; the sites were very buggy. Camp Wanapitei had run this river in lower water at least twice before our descent, so we were well-informed about potential hazards. We followed the Bazin to its mouth, where it flows into the upper Gatineau, which we followed until we reached logging roads just north of Réservoir Baskatong, a lake located northwest of Mont Laurier, 115 kilometres north of Ottawa.

Our second venture for that summer found us heading for the Magnetawan River in the Almaguin Highlands. This was a five-day trip. We used Shelagh and Jon Grant's cottage at Pointe au Baril as gathering spot and end-base camp. Our put-in was at Wahwashkesh Lake, a widening of the River. Paddling down to Georgian Bay, we took out at the mouth of the River. Altogether there were twelve of us, including ourselves and the Grants. The other eight were:

Wayman Bridge, Jim Callaghan, Hal Dickout, Dave Goslin, Dave Kirk, David Moore and Diana and Bill Paterson.

August 17, Day 3: "By Mountain Chutes"
Up about 7:00 (Shelagh and Hal much earlier) to heavy dew and to mist rising off the River. Again a clear day. Great morning vistas of this beautiful valley. Away at 8:55, shooting the first pitch easily on the far right then landing on the left. In the morning the second pitch looked much worse than it had the night before, from the heights. So we portaged left over a short near-shore trail to put in just at the lower edge of the third pitch. We paddled off in the current and into a little lake, passed two attractive lone canoeists (of the female variety) in a cedar strip and landed on Carve Island... This was a very fine, well-used campsite.

After observation from our canoes, we shot Stovepipe Rapids (class II)....Then we paddled southwest for 4 km. to Three Snye Rapids—misnamed because they are quite a spectacular falls with three channels. We portaged 300 metres on the left along a good trail

Creeping to a landing spot above a falls on the Magnetawan River.

and put into the current. After paddling 1½ km. we came to the next marked slash—another falls. Some took the portage on the right; others let down part way and carried over rocks; others let down their canoes empty in this secondary falls route on the right. Within sight of this falls is McDonald Rapids where we had lunch on the open left side while first Bruce and then many others singled the deep chute empty and on the right. Some ran it a second time. Jim and Hal tried it, taking a lot of water. Hal in the stern dropped out, and Jim paddled the heavy load to the shore. Undaunted, they did it again, successfully.

Our lunchtime continued leisurely with swims in the current and little snoozes. Finally, at 2:00 p.m., we pushed off in very high temperatures, relaxed but a bit groggy. It was less than a km. to the rapids under the CNR tracks. The portage trail on the left was in good condition, high up and over the tracks and descending steeply down to the base of the rapids (presumably the long 1,280 m. trail noted on the MNR Route, bypassing Thirty Dollar Rapids). Alas, the main pitch just before the bridge was too severe, with several holes and curves. Most of us paddled down the gorge to a bay on the left, carried the load under the bridge hard up against the abutments, lined the canoes over the big pitch and shot the lower two-thirds of the rapids. Then we loaded up, shot another enjoyable set about 150 metres downstream and camped on the right-hand sloping bank.

The cooking area was near the shore, and the tent areas were high up on the plateau. All the area was pine-clad shield country at its best—with the river really running through a gorge. We did a lot of swimming, though we were only 100 metres from the "Island" which allegedly marked the beginning

of Thirty Dollar Falls. This was pizza night. Bed
about 9:15 with high morale.

Today the Magnetawan is a very scenic river and the experience
was great fun.  At one time its waters provided the transportation
route for thousands of logs harvested by the lumbering companies
of the area and for the steamboats of the era. Today, it is a beautiful
river with a very rich history.[8]

It was, as it turned out, the southernmost river in Canada on
which the two of us were to canoe trip together—except, of course,
for our day-trip spring canoeing on many of the rivers within a three-
hour drive from Peterborough.

# 21

## RIVIÈRE NOIRE, QUÉBEC, 1986

To access the Noire, we flew into Lac Saint Patrice with First Air (with base located at Rapides des Joachims, Quebec). We paddled down Lac Saint Patrice's outlet creek to the Noire, then descended almost its full length to a road access at the power station where the River leaves the Laurentian Canadian Shield near Walthan Station. With water levels rather high, we were in for a great trip. The weather was lovely and the campsites glorious, all our participants for this year's trip were Jim Callaghan, Hal Dickout, Barry Diceman, David Goslin, Jon and Shelagh Grant, Larry Hodgins (Bruce's brother), Gwyneth Hoyle, Richard and Philip Mansfield, Ganpathy Murphy and William Taylor.

The exceptional setting contributing to tremendous morale, evident throughout the daily log:

> August 18, Day 6:
> We were up well before 7:00 to a cooler but clear day. Away by 8:45 for a 10 km. paddle to the first set, an R2 [a strong but runnable rapids], which presented no problem. Then we came to the long marked R3 [a complex rapids requiring considerable skill to run], which is really all one set, with two pitches, the first steep, and the second rocky with heavy waves. This was the location of the unclassified campsite halfway across a 200-metre portage, in the

pines on the left, a site where a previous trip had camped happily off the sand. All runs were made empty, with Bruce singling. Jim and Hal somehow tipped in the first pitch, but they portaged back up and re-ran it cleanly. Others followed, with a perfect run by Jon and Shelagh. Larry ran it three times, in turns with Bill Taylor, Dick Mansfield, and Gwyneth Hoyle. Glorious place.

Opposite are the buildings of the 50:50 Club and the small Manitou Lodge [both fish and hunt clubs]; no one was present. Carrying on, we reached the marked R3 set, which has big waves and lots of rocks. We had to keep centre, running right into the big stuff. With gear, Carol and Bruce were too far right and took in considerable water. Several had great runs, though a few portaged their gear. Larry and Bill also took water and clipped the stern of their canoe. We lunched on an attractive sandbar on river left, about 12:30.

The R3 at km 39 was very difficult. Some landed on river right, as indicated in the FQCC Report,[9]

Checking the bottom of a canoe after a run.

while some tried the left. Both had hard trails, the right-hand one thinning before the end because of several downed trees, the left-hand one full of ups and downs and a vicious hornets' nest whose inhabitants inflicted several severe bites. Bruce and Carol ran their canoe empty over the pitch on the right hand side but out from an upstream rock. Hal and Jim ran on the left, avoiding a big rock and the base of the first V; half way down is a ledge running 2/3 of the way out from the right shore. Barry and Dave also ran river right, eddied out half way, bailed and shot the lower portions. The others, reconnoitering on the left decided to haul and line the upper portion and shoot the long winding stretch below. Hal and Jim ran left all the way in Dick's canoe—Dick was suffering from a severe rear-end hornet sting. This situation made for a time-consuming delay.

The last R3 came in short order and was swift and short, with a portage on the right. Some canoes were paddled to a rock ledge at the brink, and gear and vessel hauled 15 metres over the drop; some portaged the gear to a narrow landing. Bruce ran the set empty, shooting diagonally right to left and then cutting back right. Hal and Jim and then Hal and Dick followed doubly. Larry also singled. We put into R3 water which continued for some distance. After a short pool we entered a very long meandering R2/1 section of water where the River widened and narrowed and poured over great boulder beds. Delightful.

We camped at km. 37 on a narrow, unmarked double sand site on river right, with a small sand islet off shore. With two tents on the islet, four tents on the two sandbars and three tents back in the woods, we took possession. This was done at 4:40 following a major council meeting and a consensus decision. A road ran parallel to the River back 50 metres behind us. Dinner was baked quiche with dessert of peanut butter balls. That evening Larry caught a pike, Dave a pickerel and two bass. Magnificent evening, very hard to beat. A log bridge was built out to the islet. Full moon. Many exclaimed that Day 6 on the Noire had been one of their best days ever of tripping.

The Noire was a great run, though a little short. The campsites were glorious, though some rather sandy, and the scenery was wonderful. However, in higher water levels some of these sites are under water.

Over the years we picked rivers to travel for diverse reasons, often related to long held desires of ourselves and some of our prospective companions. But we did vary, between the Near North and the Far North. Also there is a reputation concerning several of the rivers that captured our imagination. The great Quebec-side rivers of the Ottawa Valley's Near North are, northwest to southeast, Kipawa, and Dumoine (now often crowded), Noire, Rouge and Gatineau. We have paddled at least part of all these rivers, but the last two are now too populated in their lower stretches.

After our Noire run, Wanapitei's first, the route has been taken by the youth camp at least every other year. Often we blazed the way for Wanapitei, and, following this trip, the Noire was filed in Wanapitei's mental cabinet of great Near North trips.

# 22

## TWO TRIPS ON THE LADY EVELYN RIVER AND ON TO THE IVANHOE, 1987

In 1987, before heading to the Ivanhoe, we led a Lady Evelyn River Special with some of the board members of the Temagami Wilderness Society,[10] a highly charged political excursion through the threatened wilderness, as roads and clear-cutting of Old Growth Pine seemed imminent The major blockades of the Red Squirrel Road extension were only two years away. The group on this occasion included: Margaret Atwood, David Carpenter, Hon. Judy & Laurie Erola, Jess Gibson, M.T. Kelly, Diana Paterson, Joseph and Marjne Picott and Larry Scanlan. We flew into Florence Lake and descended the North Branch, the main river and the South Channel, paddling back to Camp Wanapitei. It was very hot that July, and some in the group found the pace too great and all the portages too numerous. At times morale faltered, still it was important exposure for them.

> July 12, Day 4 by Helen's Falls:
> By agreement, Judy [Erola] roused us at 6:30 a.m. and we were away well before 9:00 a.m. The rocky "rapids" between Helen's Falls and Centre Falls were too shallow to shoot, so we let down the canoes while wading in the water and negotiating the hundreds of stones. The Centre Falls carry (650 metres) went well, but we spent a good deal of time while several canoes shot the lower portion of the complex, through a

narrow cut or gorge. Margaret [Atwood] and Joe [Picott] did particularly well. Franks Falls was an easy carry and we lunched and swam on the right, about one hundred metres below the portage. Although we found bits of shade and tried to rest for an hour or so, the temperature was now at its peak for the trip. Many of us felt quite groggy.

After a lengthy discussion, we decided, by consensus, to paddle around the point and into Willow Island and take the two portages, rather than paddle north through Sucker Gut into the main part of Lady Evelyn Lake. This saves thirteen kilometres of the twenty-six involved in the long paddle round. The entire complex body of water was very low, perhaps ten feet below normal and at pre-1929 levels (pre-Matawapika Dam days), revealing a massive number of huge pine stumps and a totally eroded shoreline that afforded no nesting area for loons. Ontario Hydro clearly did not care much for either the loons or the aesthetics of wilderness travellers.[11]

The Honourable Judy Erola letting her canoe down Florence Creek.

Before reaching the first portage, we had to face a heavy south wind; we saw an osprey and met a trip of boys from Camp Onondoga [a Haliburton camp near Carnarvon] Though tired from the heat, we found the first (550 metres) carry none too difficult. But the landing at the large pond was difficult, shallow and muddy. By the time we had reached the second portage (445 metres), many of us were whacked! It begins in a moose meadow, passes through forest, and ends in a nasty one hundred metres of huge rocks and a shallow put-in. A few had to make three trips.

The south end of the main part of Lady Evelyn Lake is island-strewn and very beautiful. We landed at the marked high rock campsite on the main island about 7:00 p.m. Setting up camp was slow, but we nevertheless had libations and a huge baked pizza feed engineered by Judy, Carol and Diana. Thunderstorms threatened from the south, but they passed to the east or west. Margaret then informally led a long "camp singsong" especially designed for the child in us all. It was great fun. Terry was particularly Irish! Bed well after dark and in high spirits.

In the autumn of 1989 there were large road blockades and many police arrests. The first blockade was by the Temagami Wilderness Society and the second by the TAA (Teme Augama Nishnabai), however, the road was completed. But only one truck ever drove its length. The uproar was so great, that the central part through the Lady Evelyn watershed was never used and has become impassable. The TAA now have a draft agreement, but minor issues raised by federal officials seem to be delaying a final vote.

The following week Bruce and Ted Moores (with spouse Janny Padelford) led a second group on the Lady Evelyn River. It was a Wanapitei Reunion Trip, mainly with alumni from around 1960: Judy Cairns, Tom Cobean, Scotty LaRue and wife Emily and Paul Richmond. The group flew into Florence Lake and paddled the North Branch, the main portion and the South Channel, paddling back to Wanapitei. Lots of shared fun and reflection as noted in this journal excerpt:

> July 22, Day 6:
>
> This morning we undertook the Fat Man's Portage or Squeeze, with its steep, narrow and rocky descent, and passed downstream, shooting and lining a few shallows, to the site of the Old Barn, now just a memory with a few bits of timber, by the shallow rapids. Lots of pictures. Then it was on to Willow Island Lake and over the two carries into Lady Evelyn Lake. We lunched at the high campsite on the south end of the main body of this Lake [where Bruce and Carol and the TWS group) had camped ten days earlier]. We paddled on to the short carry into Diamond Lake. In Diamond, the first five of our projected campsites were taken by other groups.
>
> We camped on the high site, on the south-end island as a storm threatened but failed to materialize. Marcus Bruce [a veteran Wanapitei tripper and for a time Assistant Director, long a Board Member and currently the Camp Treasurer] flew in to join us for dinner and the night. Glorious evening. Many slept under the stars.

What a tremendous reunion trip we had, packed with such fun and so many reminiscences. Ted, though then living in Minneapolis, soon rejoined the Wanapitei Board and later became its chair.

Our third group for the year rallied in mid-August at Ivanhoe Provincial Park near Foleyet, a small village southwest of Timmins, and in the morning made our way in two vehicles, southwest past Chapleau, then southeast (about fifty kilometres) to the tiny settlement of Kormak just before Sultan.

We followed tiny streams including the Kinogami, into the Ivanhoe River, descending it northward back to Ivanhoe Park, a campground). We had magnificent canoe sails (in two rigs), involving racing three boats against four boats. In spite of low water, we, in fact moved much more quickly than the two Wanapitei youth groups that had covered the route in 1982 and 1984. With time to spare, most of us car-carried our canoes to River Valley and spent a solid day on the Temagami River, paddling and portaging up several sets and then shooting downstream.

> August 12, Day 6:
> Up at 7:00 a.m. and away by 8:30, following a granola breakfast, paddling in a light following wind to a "gorp" break at 9:30. Then we rigged sails— two rafts, one with four canoes (Jim Callaghan/ Hal Dickout, Bill Cormode/David Webber, Bruce/ Carol, and Dave Goslin/Barry Diceman) and one with three (Daryl Hodgins/Divya Bhatia, Bill Paterson/Diana and Ken Shonk/Shelagh Grant). We all used paddles for masts. The wind increased, and it became very exciting as we found our way downstream. The three-canoe raft was slightly faster.

Shelagh, wearing a bathing suit, donated an item of clothing, which was erected in jest as a "turbo bra," serving as a mizzen sail. The foursome used a stern-stay system, and when "reaching," inserted two paddles deep into the water as centreboards. The threesome stopped for lunch at a tree-house by Ivanhoe Cabin No. I on the right, but the lunch was with the "raft" behind. While waiting for the other "raft," they sat around a table by the cabin and appeared to be in the middle of a bridge game when the others arrived.

Wanagans were opened and Carol prepared lunch; then all gathered to laugh, to eat and to relax.

Sailing with Dr. Jim Callaghan who was checking the river ahead.

After lunch came the long reach and the long twisty stretch before the Lake proper. We sailed all the turns, with only a little help from a paddle. With the foursome getting a head start, Jim stood amidships, eyeglass in one hand and the other on the mast, making rude comments about low morale amongst the crew of the threesome. Great fun—about 35 km. of sailing.

We finally lowered sails about ½ km. from the Park beach. We obtained sites close to those we had used at the beginning of the trip. Dinner of bulgar and dal sauce at dusk. Meanwhile Bruce, Daryl, Divya and Gos engaged in the Kormak shuttle for the other cars, which took four hours. We had lots of talk concerning our next move. The Spanish and Lower Temagami received attention and several phone calls were made. Bed quite late.

We did have fun on the Ivanhoe, but the water levels in the upper reaches of the Ivanhoe were really too low. Fortunately, the one day of sailing and the one day for most participants on the Temagami River produced a great memorable experience. We would not rerun the Ivanhoe.

# 23

## ONLY DAY PADDLING, 1988

There was no canoe trip for us in 1988. Bruce was critically ill with multiple pulmonary emboli. Although under investigation it was not yet diagnosed, when he had a massive attack while at Wanapitei over New Years. Over an eight-month period he was in three different hospitals for a total of ten weeks. Following high-risk surgery in August, at UCSD (University California San Diego) he made a miraculous recovery. In late September, during the Trent Canadian Studies visit to Wanapitei, he was able to get into a canoe.

We were to have led a two-week trip in August, but instead our son Geoff and his wife Pat Bowles co-led the trip that we had planned. It was an exciting voyage in northeastern Ontario on the remote Kattawagami River to James Bay.

# 24

## THE LADY EVELYN RIVER REUNION, 1989

Primarily this was an adult reunion trip for friends (and cousin Daryl and Barbara Hodgins) who had travelled with us many times. Unfortunately, Carol had a back fracture and other injuries sustained in a June car accident and probably should not have joined the trip at all. However, she (Carol) did fly in to Macpherson Lake on the Lady Evelyn River from Camp Wanapitei with the group and stayed at the upper-end quartzite campsite while most of the group portaged up the Seven Sisters for lunch and then portaged or shot the rapids back down to the campsite.

The next morning we paddled and portaged down past Shangra-La to Divide (Katherine) Lake, where a bush plane picked Carol up and flew her back to Camp. The group then went up into adjacent Dry Lake, climbed the rather difficult Dry Lake Ridge, returned to Divide and then descended the South Channel to Willow Island, Lady Evelyn and Diamond lakes, and thus back to Wanapitei.

A note from the log records: "Under the circumstances and with our deepest thanks, Barb Hodgins and Lynda Mason became 'Master-Cooks-in-Training' for this gourmet special. They more than passed with flying colours."

> July 19, Day 4: "Dry Lake and Ridge"
> Dick Mansfield agreed to guard the site and "write."
> Don and Lynda Mason, Bruce, [along with] Greg
> Taylor, took Carol and our dog Kandy down to

Divide (Katherine) Lake for the rendezvous with the Cessna. The plane came at noon. Meanwhile the others had portaged one canoe from the pool below Shangra-La, 445 m. on a rough tract up to the outlet swamp of Dry Lake. Tom Morley, on his carry, snapped the stern thwart bolts and rivets on his canoe and fell k'boom!

Then he, Barb and Daryl and Renata Hulley paddled to the beautiful far, north-side campsite on Dry Lake. Tom came back, standing as in the African Queen above the swamps, for Gord Peck and Graham Hulley, arriving as the rest came back from the Cessna fly-off with a second canoe. When we approached the lunch site, the other three were very busy "flashing," quick nude swimming. After lunch, Graham, Tom, Bruce and Gordon set off for the summit of the quartzite Dry Lake Ridge. MNR had marked a trail on some maps, but it was only occasionally visible on the ground. Anyway, we went up over an Esker, cut north (left), climbed high through thick white pine forests (biggest had a 3 m. circumference) with underbrush, to the bare rock face. Graham went straight up. Tom found a more circuitous, gentler route to the south, which Bruce and Gordon followed. We reached the highest spot on that ridge, though another to the west looked slightly higher and ran about one kilometre to the north. Another year if we climb here we will take more time. The view south and east was magnificent. We clearly saw Maple Mountain and the eastern shore of Lady Evelyn Lake and some far off clear-cuts. Southward we saw the lake which was the source of the Wakimika (higher than Dry Lake). Ascent 1½ hours; descent ¾ of an hour, going due south, off the ridge and down to a marsh that was the Lake's inflow creek. We picked up from there,

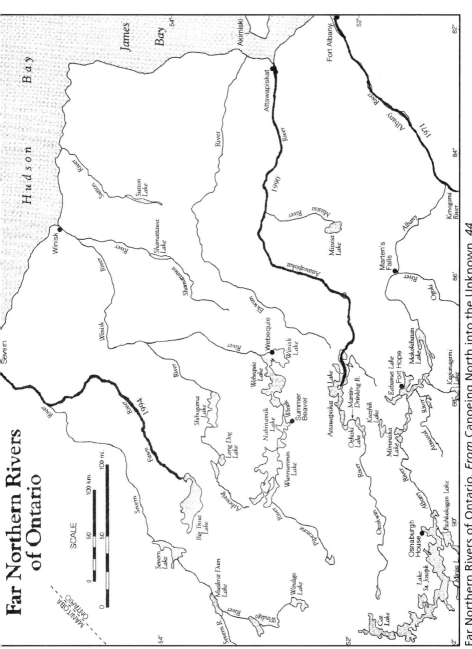

Far Northern Rivers of Ontario. *From* Canoeing North into the Unknown, *44.*

the MNR "trail" and followed it until the Esker. Some stayed back and tried but caught no fish in the shallow Lake water. We left for the portage in two shifts. Back at Shangra-La, Dick had started dinner of "gado gado."[12] Bed by 10:00 p.m.

This Lady Evelyn trip was truly a great reunion excursion of friends. Carol was extremely sorry not be able to continue on it. She really should not have even flown in for the two nights. However, she had planned the menu and wanted to be of some help. The scenery is so beautiful, and with the wonderful weather our energetic group was able to enjoy some fantastic hiking, as well as paddling.

On the final morning, the great Dr. Tom Morley, currently our eldest tripper, following a morning dip, marched up to the campfire and stood "spread eagled," with arms above his head and announced that this was his final canoe trip, and that we were all such wonderful friends, but rather crazy. In November 2007, Tom, now in his late eighties, is still alive, but sadly Dr. Graham Hulley and Lynda Mason are not.

# PART FOUR:

# NEAR AND FAR,
# NORTH AND SOUTH, 1990–1999

# 25
## DOWN THE ATTAWAPISKAT RIVER TO JAMES BAY, 1990

This was Wanapitei's first adult trip on the Attawapiskat. Also known as the Otoskwin-Attawapiskat, this is a major, very long river running from west to east in a very wiggly line across most of Northern Ontario, with the name change at the lake where we put in. It enters James Bay opposite the very large Akimiski Island (Nunavut) half way up the James Bay coast. Nearly all Attawapiskat Village inhabitants are Cree. Recently, just north of the lower part of the river, the area has become the focal point for major diamond mining activity.

It had already been run at least three times by Wanapitei's older youth campers, including one co-led by our son Shawn. We ran the River from Lansdowne House, a former HBC post, on Lake Attawapiskat to the village on the James Bay coast. The ten of us had a most wonderful time—Ted and Bill Cormode, Cathryn Rees, Jon and Shelagh Grant, Graham and Renate Hulley, and Chris Sergeant; most were friends of long standing, two were recent.

We rallied in Timmins and flew into Lansdowne House although the canoes had to be flown in from Pickle Lake, almost four hundred kilometres north and slightly west of Thunder Bay. The three Wanapitei youth trips that had already paddled the River, put in a little north of the Lake onto the Otoskwin River and paddled east, first to Lansdowne House. After flowing through Shield country, with the usual rapids and boreal forest, the Attawapiskat River enters into the broad James Bay Lowlands and is soon travelling through magnificent, eroded, beautiful limestone banks and cliffs and dropping over long, runable rapids, as the size of the spruce on the shore shrink and thin out. This was a truly spectacular area of the River.

> August 21, Day 11: "Finally, the Rapids of the Three Limestone Gorges."
> Up just after 6:00, away by 8:00. One hour downstream, we paddled past the Cree party camped on the right, cooking breakfast. They waved. We should have landed, and would have, save for the presence of Atta, our very thin little dog found under a tent floor at an abandoned Cree camp, about halfway through our trip abandoned. Had we done the right thing? [most of us felt the dog would otherwise die.] Clearly they had not gone up to the Missisa River and presumably had no link with that goose camp [where Atta was found] or whatever there. Clearly the group in the boat were checking their own fish nets.
>
> Now onto the last of our 1:50,000 maps. We finally approached the First Gorge, at a point where the River turns sharply to the south as it cuts through the limestone ridges, amidst a maze of high-cliffed little islands. We stopped and carefully read the trip reports of both Marcus Bruce ('78) and Shawn Hodgins ('81) about the forthcoming complex run through the Rapids; the former trip ran in high water and the latter in low.
>
> We entered the gorge starting moderately left of centre. Then we worked our way through this intriguing maze, following what we thought was the main current, winding gorgeously amidst wonderful rapids that come in three sections. The channels are many, and some have inadequate water in them and must be avoided. Several bowpersons stopped paddling in brief

quieter moments to take pictures. Then we eddied out right, on a tiny beach, for more pics, relaxation and a climb up the adjacent limestone hill for better views, across and down—Atta, the dog made it too.

Then it was off for 15 km. to the Second Gorge in the cluster of islands by the two marked "Rs" on the map. This gorge was even more spectacular than the first, with even more diverse channels. We ran basically down the main right-hand course, watching to try not to swing up a quiet cut rather than down a main one. Frequently the pitch was rather heavy, two in particular. We landed on a significant looking beach on the left for lunch. Behind the narrow beach lay a spruce-wooded knoll with a magnificent viewpoint. We swam. We ate. We relaxed. It was very hot for far Northern Ontario, at 53° North, in late August.

In the afternoon we paddled for more than two hours almost to the next and single "R" on the map. We saw a bear along the right bank bound out of the shallows, dripping water, and bound off into the poplar brush. Where some tiny islands exist, we came rather suddenly to a pitch, between the mainland and one such island. We could see several different chutes.The entire area was now island-studded, mostly spruce-covered, above limestone banks. [The distance] between this pitch and the Third Gorge was about one kilometre. The Third Gorge is beautiful, but less spectacular than the previous two. The pitches are, however, more severe, especially the second one. If it had been July, with high water, one route could have been too severe and thus require finding alternate secondary paths through the islands, as Marcus' report discussed. We paddled right over a high shallow ledge which had no real "V," only a place with more water. This required a hard thrust after the pitch, to clear the hole and shallows.

A kilometre past the Gorge, we camped on the left bank, along the straight narrower northeast stretch. We had been watching billowy smoke clouds on the southeast sky—with clear horizon points. How far off we could not tell. Dinner of tabouli with cauliflower and broccoli sauce. Again, today we had canoed 52 km.

The large Cree village of Attawapiskat is on the broad estuary of the River just upstream from its mouth, at above 53° North latitude. Looking for a campsite, we wandered around the community and met many of the people. We were allowed to camp in the churchyard. It was across from a small hospital, and we were allowed to use the bathrooms there. Bruce and Jon stayed to look after the gear, but Jon arranged for a local Cree, Marius Kataqupit, to take the rest of us out in his freight canoe to view the open James Bay.

In the distance was Akimiski, the largest island in James Bay. Now part of Nunavut, it is a migratory bird sanctuary for Canada geese, American and Black ducks, Marbled Godwits and other shore

Cathyrn Rees talking to Cree children in Attawapiskat.

birds. Unfortunately, we did not have the time to go to the Island.

Overall the trip was a most memorable, high morale experience, but we certainly could have used two or three more days. Our fourteen days included one for flying in and one for flying out. The Attawapiskat was probably our best far Northern Ontario trip. We came together as a group, experienced much and learned a lot. Bill Cormode and Cathryn Rees later became partners and have become very close friends with us.

We stealthfully (though one flight attendant knew) took little Atta, the dog, with us on the flights from Attawapiskat to Moosonee and then to Timmins. Graham and Renata then took Atta in the car with them to Wanapitei, and then home to Ottawa. With the Hulleys she lived happily and, expensively, for the rest of her natural life.

# 26

## THE SOUTH MACMILLAN-PELLY RIVERS TRIP
## IN THE YUKON, 1991

The Aboriginal Peoples who have lived in at least the lower portions of the Macmillan and Pelly are Northern Tuchone. People of the same tribal group also live around Carmacks and Mayo in the central Yukon. Those of the lower Pelly and Macmillan have a permanent village at Pelly Crossing. The community is officially called the Fort Selkirk Band or the T'seki Huch'an. Fort Selkirk itself is now without residents and is located just downstream from the Crossing, where the Pelly joins the Yukon River; it was established by Robert Campbell of the HBC in 1848. The Tuchone call the lower Pelly the T'seki Netu and the main Macmillan the Khro Tu.

In 1840, Robert Campbell of the HBC became the first European to reach the Pelly River. He paddled from the upper Liard, up its tributary the Frances, which he named, and the Finlayson, crossing the divide at what became Campbell Creek and onto the Pelly where, in 1846, he established the Pelly Banks Post that would survive until 1849. He named the river after Sir John Henry Pelly (1777–1852), London Governor of the HBC. In 1843, Campbell descended the Pelly and named the Macmillan (the mouth of which he passes) after Chief Factor James Macmillan, his immediate superior, at Fort Garry on the Red River.[1]

Besides Bruce and Carol, this extraordinary trip involved Myk and Doreen Bartlett, Bill Cormode, Cathryn Rees, Elliot and Meredith Rodger, Kirsten Franklin and Michael Watts. We knew them all very well and had already paddled with most of them. After flying to Whitehorse, we were taken in a van with our canoes (an adventure in itself) all the way north through the mountains, past the Ross River Bridge and up what had been the World War Two Canol Road to Norman Wells, for the Petroleum Pipeline.[2] We put into the South Macmillan River on our left, not a long distance before the Canol Road crosses the divide into the Northwest Territories and then becomes only a very rough trail. Soon the River leaves the Road flows westerly. We followed it down past its merger with the North Macmillan and, some travel days later, its merger with the Pelly River. We followed the large Pelly River to Pelly Crossing, where the Whitehorse-Dawson highway crosses the River, before it enters the Yukon River. For most of the journey we paddled through awesome mountain scenery. The weather had been and, for a time, continued warm and dry. We saw small forest fires and even hiked through a smouldering area. Then came the rain and more rain.

The trip through Chipewyan-Dene Country was most exhilarating as shown in these excerpts from our log:

Our van and canoes on the cable ferry crossing the Pelly River, while driving on the Canol Road.

July 12, Day 4:

….The next stretch of 13 kilometres was very exciting and now in high water, quite challenging. Myk calculated the drop at 20 feet per mile with some steeper stretches. "R. Jordan, in 1985, claimed the drop to be 35 feet per mile. It was here in this stretch that the Arch Jones party in 1990 had a dump and mishap."[3] With a few minor troubles, everyone made it through the fast water, diverse pitches, many side ledges, lots of rocks, shoreline sweepers etc. Often we stopped in eddies for breath and bailing… During the afternoon we paddled for about 2 ½ hours, seeing seven moose (two cows with a calf each, two single cows and one big bull moose), a bald eagle, several beaver, and great vistas.

July 14, Day 6:

…. In the afternoon we reached the confluence of the South and North Macmillan, stopping at the merger point to examine a trapper's cabin. Then it was on to Russell Creek, which entered from the right or north bank. There at "Armstrong's Landing" just after the mouth, we met a key family of the small "Christian community," Lee and Mary Persinger and their two children, David and Benji plus the mother; [we also met] Mary Carpenter of the second family and their visiting granny. Mary's husband Bud was in Whitehorse arranging to move there because their son needed to attend Grade X, at the high school there.

They had a small vegetable farm, and they had seriously trapped, but the recent collapse in fur prices (and the anti-fur campaign) had effectively destroyed this part of their livelihood along with that of many others in the North, both Aboriginal and Euro-Canadian. At Armstrong they also made and sold (and marketed throughout the Yukon) fur and wooden handicrafts and artwork. They also catered to trippers, charging a bit for tent sites, sauna etc. They also helped horse outfitters who swim their steeds from off the distant Canol Road, across the Macmillan River and up the Russell Valley for late summer-autumn hunting of moose or sheep. They either fly out and in by sea plane or use a powerful outboard for this very long (taking over 12 hours) trip to Pelly Crossing; neither woman had done the latter, though they had lived here many years.

These were the first people we had seen since leaving the van. We camped on the site provided. We cooked dinner and washed up, using their drying house; some used the sauna. We spent the evening in their lodge, chatting, eating popcorn and drinking buckets of tea, Wonderful hospitality. Bed about 10:30. It rained most of the night.

July 16, Day 8:
Again the water rose about half a metre during the night, bringing levels to a very high point indeed. Up at 7:00 a.m., and away at 9:30 to a warm day, one for shorts and T-shirts. The valley gradually opened up, with high peaks on both sides, with Dromedary Mountain soon visible to the southwest and sharp pointed Clark Peak (or Storybook Mountain) to the north, as named by George McConnell of the Geological Survey of Canada in 1902: the latter (Clark Peak) is part of the great Kalzas Range running alongside the north bank…

July 20, Day 12: "The Granite Canyon of the Pelly— and the Hike"
Up again to rain at 7:30. Slow, long breakfast. Then we spent a couple of hours making spray covers,

bow and centre, from ground sheets, and the orange plastic tarp, with help from some light rope. Away at 10:40.

Through the Granite Canyon by 12:20, that is in one-and-a-half hours, amid drizzle and lots of eddy stops. Basically we ran river-left, until just before the hard right turn preceding Needle Rock Island, in mid-river, where we cut to the right side and eddied out. We had very high waves, in our extremely high water, on the outside first two curves. At the second one, that is just before we cut to the right side using upstream ferries, we had to go into three or four substantial waves (say one-and-a-half metres tall), high and long and relatively smooth.

The Bartletts were slightly closer to the centre than the rest of us, and Doreen thus sustained a very large face-full of water and the front half of their canoe rose very far out of the water. Some took no water at all. Edging close around that right turn, in full view of Needle Rock, we passed the Island close by on its right. We could equally have been close to it on the left at that spot. With the drizzle over, we landed around another modest left bend, on the left bank, at the upstream side of the mouth of Needlerock Creek. Here there is an old cabin and a trail up the valley of the Creek and onto the ridge. It is also an official campsite and trail of the Yukon government.

We set up camp, had lunch and started off on a hike up to the ridge, then up the Pelly Valley for a kilometre or so. [There was the most beautiful smell in the air; we soon realized the side of the hill was completely covered with wild sage.] Magnificent vistas. Michael and Cathryn went on for some time, as the ridge wound back and forth, till they could see and photo the Rock; they were gone three hours.

The Bartletts followed the trail up the Creek portion of the ridge. According to the official sign, the trail goes for a long way indeed, ultimately away up the Pelly Valley.

Back at the beautiful campsite, some fished in the clear creek, some read, some washed and some cooked. Elliot caught a large whitefish and a larger northern pike. Bruce's "got away." The best spot was where the clear water of the Creek met the very murky water of the Pelly. In lovely weather we had a huge, slow dinner, including the fish. Morale was very high. At 9:00 we had a brief shower after the sky clouded over. It had been a tremendous day, though we had only covered 10 km. It rained off and on during the night.

July 21, Day 13:
Up at 7:00, and away by 9:20. The weather was good and we were paddling in fast big water. We stopped when we saw racks of fish drying up on top of the right bank. It was the first fish camp we had seen, so we stopped and went up, where we met George Johny who was living there with his large family and the Alfreds, and his grandfather and grandmother. We met some more members of the family. We exchanged some of our hot chocolate etc. for some dried salmon. The camp had rough road access to Pelly Crossing. Here we learned that George and his son had indeed shot a moose upriver—we saw some of the [moose] quarters. On the day of our hike we had heard the sound of the shot and of the outboard motor....

This was one of our memorable trips. We had a great group and the scenery was spectacular. We also had more reports than usual, both published and in typescript from those who had gone before;

three were from the early years of the twentieth century. Since 1991, there has been one other Wanapitei trip following the South Macmillan portion, a Voyageur youth trip that then travelled up the North Macmillan and beyond.

# 27

## ON THE CLEARWATER RIVER IN NORTHERN
## SASKATCHEWAN AND ALBERTA, 1992

Besides Bruce and Carol, this year's main trip included Myk and Doreen Bartlett, Andy Carron, Michael Watts and Bev Wilson. The two of us plus Michael, Myk and Doreen gathered at the University of Alberta in Edmonton, while Bev and Andy were picked up at Meadow Lake, Saskatchewan. Myk was a student working on his PhD in engineering and had made all the travel and rental arrangements including the van, trailer and drivers. We were taken to the put-in, along with the canoes that had been rented from the University of Alberta Outdoor Education Centre

We drove the long haul to the northeast into Saskatchewan, north past Meadow Lake all the way to Lloyd Lake Landing on the very upper reaches of the Clearwater River. After paddling down the remote stretches of the Clearwater and after leaving the Canadian Shield, we passed the northern end of the famous Methye[4] Portage (the great watershed portage of the fur trade from 1778 to 1886, linking the source of the Churchill River at Lac La Loche to the Clearwater-Athabaska Country). Continuing westward, we descended the Clearwater into Alberta down to Fort McMurray of Tar Sands fame, where the Clearwater enters the Athabaska. This marked the end of our journey. We were then picked up and driven back to Edmonton.

> July 16, Day 10: "Below Contact Rapids, past the Methye Portage Landing, and into Alberta"

Up after 7:00, except for Bev who rose earlier and speeded up the process. Away at 9:10 in light rain. Lunched at 1:10 p.m. in very light current. Before then we had stopped briefly to chat with two La Loche Dene camped on the left in their V-stern canoe with an outboard lying inside. Using an ATV, they had entered the Clearwater off an old logging road of the 1950s, just below Contact Rapids. This track comes in from La Loche village. We had seen no evidence of any logging; it must have been old and back in, south of the River. They were hunting moose.

We reached the north end of the Methye Portage at 2:00 p.m. We hiked up the steep trail to the famous Lookout and beyond, to the indistinct divide between the Clearwater and the Churchill watersheds (the great divide between the Hudson Bay watershed and the Mackenzie watershed, the old pre-1870 border between Rupert's Land and the Northwestern Territory. There is no view at the divide itself. We took pictures at the Lookout and on our descent examined the deep ruts, in the trail

Myk and Doreen Bartlett are seen leaving the campsite on the first day of paddling, after a long drive from Edmonton.

of the Methye Portage.  The ruts were made after 1850, when ox carts and pack horses were used to carry most of the goods over this great "Portage," so vital to everyone remotely linked to the northeastern fur trade or exploration in that period.

We were back at the Landing by 4:10 p.m.; this Landing is in a big grassy field. The trail beginning from the northern upstream end, is wet and bushy for the first half kilometre, then excellent. It climbs steeply through mainly poplar growth and shows evidence of current snowmobile use. Using the old logging road, the River, the Methye and Lac La Loche would make a great winter circle route out of the village. We hiked it in intermittent drizzle.

Then we paddled the 10 km. or so into Alberta, stopping after about a kilometre at a narrow spruce and Jack pine grove up a low sandy bank on the left. There we found two excellent cabins back in the bush, owned, as we were later told, by a Fort McMurray trapper. A good winter trail headed west— it was 7:00 p.m.

While we were on the Methye, the two Dene had passed us, then we had passed them hunting. Now they came along, dropped in and visited. Then they fastened on their motor and headed back upstream. They did not hunt in Alberta. They told us that the trail led west to Fort McMurray. Shortly after, we heard a gunshot upstream. We set up camp and cooked a huge dinner, outside, near the cabins in a fire pit.

The Clearwater trip complemented our 1977 trip on the upper Churchill River. Besides being a wonderful challenging trip in its own right, the Clearwater, especially from the Methye Portage downstream, is so full of significant classic Canadian fur trade history, exploration and the field work of the Geological Survey.

Alexander Mackenzie, HBC Governor George Simpson, John Franklin, George Back and all the others passed over the Methye and down the Clearwater. Imagine the stories that Trail could tell if only it could talk.

# 28

## TO THE SOPER OR KUUJUAQ RIVER
## ON BAFFIN ISLAND, 1993

This was the first of three Arctic voyages which we would lead on the Soper or Kuujuaq River on Baffin Island, which is now part of Nunavut. Bill Cormode and Cathryn Rees, Jon and Shelagh Grant, Elliot and Meredith Rogers, Ken Shonk and son Kevin, Michael Watts and Bev Wilson were with us. This canoe trip was one where there was a lot of exceptional hiking.

From  Iqaluit we flew west, in Twin Otters, across Frobisher Bay and the large peninsula, Terra Incognito, named by Martin Frobisher in 1576. We landed on "the Esker," the only place in the upper River where planes could land east across the River from Mount Joy. This mountain, which then and in later times we would alway climb, was named after Alfred Herbert Joy, an important early Mounted Police officer on Baffin Island.

Bush flight and other arrangements were made by Matty McNair of North Winds Arctic Adventures. In 1989 our son Geoff and wife Pat Bowles, who were working in Iqaluit at that time, were part of a group organized by Brent Boddy and Jane Cooper, acquaintances of Geoff and Pat. Their trip was the second kayak or canoe group to paddle the Soper River from the mouth of the Cascade River. The first trip had been in 1983. That initial recreational paddle led to ours and to all other recreational canoe trips on the Soper. Of course, the Inuit had already been running round-trip snowmobile races all the way from Kimmirut, up the Soper, across Terra Incognita and across Frobisher Bay on the ice, and back following an overnight.

Our log begins with our first paddling of the trip:

August 12, Day 3: "From Panorama Flats to the Cascade Flats"
[our first paddling after the arrival and hiking days]
Up around 7:00 a.m. to a mixed sky and cooler temperatures. We slowly loaded our canoes, 200 metres downstream from our campsite by the Esker. Away at 9:30 in very shallow water, necessitating "in-and-outs" for about three kilometres, more out than in, with lots of wading. We lifted over a one-metre ledge on the right, the left of the little island being too shallow, but perhaps a runable shoot in higher water. Then we passed a park shelter (mainly for winter use) on river left, a point already reached by a film crew for the Canadian Heritage Rivers System [CHRS]. They were walking along the riverbank. The crew, which was guided by our friend Max Finkelstein, a CHRS employee, had only one small inflated raft for the five of them. They had what looked like a tonne of equipment (part of which had been flown in with us on our third flight). Lots of caribou and no more wading.

We ran two sets of rapids (class "1½") amid light rain, the last just before the confluence with the Joy River, running down along the west side of Mount Joy, which was now centre spot directly behind us. We disembarked on the right bank of the full River, while we enjoyed the beautiful warm weather. Then the entire film crew arrived, all in their heavily loaded single raft. We took pictures of them as they filmed the many caribou and the scenes up both valleys and back to the Mountain, a scene we will long remember. Then we pushed on, not knowing that we would not again be talking to the film crew until Lake Harbour.

Soon we came to a class 2+ rapid requiring shore examination on river left. We ran through a narrow channel left of centre, lunching then on the right bank past the last "R" of Soper on the map (N. Grid 08). After lunch the current in the river increased, with many light rapids in restricted sections, involving small gorges. We ran a two kilometre, complex set almost all the way to the mouth of the Cascade River on river left. There we examined the large flat on the left where two branches of the Cascade enter the Soper; we found out later that this was where Geoff Hodgins, Pat Bowles, Jane Cooper, etc. had landed on their 1989 kayak trip and was now deemed too unsafe for such plane landings!

During our examination the wind increased to a rather high velocity, so we decided that the opposite shore [west side that is river right] looked somewhat more sheltered. That is where we set up camp, finding a "bunker" near the River for cooking and eating. Cathryn, Bev and Mike recrossed the River to the east side and hiked beyond the flats and up the Cascade valley, far past the falls visible from the Soper, up the steep valley past two more falls, one being very high and perhaps the "95 foot" one mentioned in the original Dewey Soper literature (from 1931). Ken, Kevin, Carol and Jon climbed and walked the ridge behind our campsite.

During a light rain, we cooked a dinner of beef stew with mixed vegetables, putting up the big blue tarp on Carol's suggestion, with engineering advice supplied by Bill. There were, of course, no trees. We could see, in the distance behind us, by the narrows of the last pitch of rapids, the film crew, now camped. Meredith and Elliot also climbed the ridge and saw two hikers with a dog, [across the River] walking far downstream on the left bank. We went to bed early, after watching many caribou amid increasing rain.

Aug. 13, Day 4 "To and at the Junction of the Livingstone":

Although we got up before 7:00 a.m., very heavy wind hit about 7:15 and virtually blew down two of the non-dome tents. So we had a big rush to take down all tents before breakfast. We were away about 9:30 against strong south winds in our faces. Near the mouth at Willow Creek (a creek with a small willow growth) we came upon a locked "Group Shelter," set up by Park authorities, on river left where only the sturdy and stylish outhouse toilets were open. The rain was heavy. Then at N. Grid 023 by Mount Moore (535 metres) to the east, we caught up with the "two hikers with a dog," at their campsite. They were Virginia (Lavin) and John Moss who previously had encouraged us to paddle the Soper when they were at a Canoeing Symposium at Wanapitei in September 1992, and again when we met them at the WCA (Wilderness Canoeing Symposium[5]) in January 1993.

John (and Jack, the dog) had been on the Itijjagiaq Trail since July 18, when he had been taken across Frobisher Bay (when the Bay broke up) to the Meta Incognita Peninsula shore where the long, very rough trail up and over the ridges to Mount Joy begins. He had since been hiking and writing. Virginia had been brought up from the village of Lake Harbour to the Group shelter by an outboard freight canoe about two weeks before our meeting. The key needed for the shelter was on the wall of the cabin's garbage bin. John was researching major articles on the Trail and the River Valley. (The "Trail" is really an unmarked route, not a pathway.)

We now had really very strong south winds against us, as well as cold rain. So the four-kilometre paddle to the mouth of the Livingstone[6] (river right) was quite difficult, despite the confusing current and light rapids acting in our favour. It was the hardest hour of the trip. Yet clearly the water level on the Soper was rising, and it was rising very fast. We set up camp on the lower "lawn bank" of the Livingstone's right or south shore, on a lengthy flat occasionally used as a landing strip for people only travelling the lower River. Amid showers, we ate lunch and rested.

In the afternoon, the weather improved, the sky partially cleared and the temperature rose—as did our spirits. Most of us hiked upstream on the Livingstone (or Katingniq) and most of us passed the magnificent 100-metre wide falls, ten metres high. Several went much further; Bev and Cathryn passed many more rapids and at least two large falls.

The Livingstone River was running fast, furious and high. We all saw lots of caribou. Carol and the Grants saw 21 caribou cross the Livingstone from the north side. More followed, all moving south. Kevin, Ken and Elliot fished without luck. John, Virginia and Jack were seen across the Soper, and we ferried them over to our side to join us; the disadvantage of the trail route is that hikers can really explore only on one side of the valley below Mount Joy. We all had dinner together and camped together. Great fun and great talks, again with the tarp up and amid almost constant rain. We did go to bed relatively early. Well after midnight the wind swung to the northwest, roaring down the Livingstone valley, shaking all the tents and ripping the Grant's Eureka three-four person timberline very severely, causing them quite a wet night.

Cathryn Rees, Bev Wilson, Bill Cormode and Michael Watts, en route with an Inuit fisherman, heading down the fjord to Hudson Strait to view icebergs.

We paddled the Soper River all the way down to Soper Lake and across to a landing where there is a road into the coastal Inuit hamlet of Kimmirut, formerly Lake Harbour, at the head of a fjord. In Kimmirut we enjoyed the exceptional hospitality of the residents, went out on their large outboards with cabins, and down the barren fjord into Hudson Strait to view the icebergs and seals. On our return part way up the fjord, we stopped on the barren shore for lunch provided by the Inuit boat drivers.

Both the Soper River and Lake were named after J. Dewey Soper, born in 1906. A skilled naturalist, he made at least two trips to southern Baffin Island, the first in 1923 and the second in 1930–31. As well as other explorations, he fully explored the River that soon was to bear his name; he also conducted a faunal study. The Inuit are succeeding in having the name of the River changed back to Kuujuak "Big River" and the Lake to Tasiujajuaq "Big Lake." The entire valley is now a Nunavut Territorial Park called Katannilik, "the place of the waterfalls." The River has been designated part of the Canadian Heritage Rivers System.

Bruce published an article entitled "Soper River: Baffin Island Enchantment."[7] The article concludes with the following:

> "The Soper. Not a difficult trip, not a trying trip, a warm then a cool trip—perhaps we were a bit late in the season—an Arctic trip with the caribou, in a fantastic landscape, and all with friends, visitors and through Inuit lands."[7]

We would return to the Soper for two more great canoe trips, one in 1996 and one in 2001.

# 29

## ON THE FAWN-SEVERN RIVER TO HUDSON BAY, 1994

The northern Severn River to Fort Severn on Hudson Bay is as far north as one can get in Ontario (56° N). From offshore you can virtually see the Manitoba coast. We flew in from Pickle Lake, in single-engine Otters, to the Cree Village of Angling Lake, just east of Big Trout. We then descended the Fawn River for ten days to its junction with the broader island-strewn Severn itself. From there it took three days to reach Hudson Bay. This was Wanapitei's first and, so far only, trip on the northern Severn. Along with Bruce and Carol, the group involved Bill Cormode, Cathryn Rees, Tom Romans, Fred Emmings and Michael Watts.

Clearly the route had been used by York Boats of the Hudson's Bay Company during the 1840s. York Boats largely replaced the "36 foot" canots de maître (or Montreal canoes), carrying furs downstream and supplies and trade goods upstream. York Boats were long, flat, bottom-planked boats that were rowed rather than paddled; they even had a large square sail and mast that could be raised when there was a significant tail wind. The York Boat was hauled or dragged over portages, which usually had logs on the ground placed crossways to the line of travel.

We left the Shield on our fourth day of paddling and entered the broad Hudson Bay Lowlands. Throughout this route the great spruce forests dominate, with the size and forest density decreasing radically as the Bay is approached. It is full-scale tundra on the coast. It had been dry and forest fires were burning in the vicinity. Old dying fires right beside us on our second last day. The earlier Shield section of the river had the expected runable rapids, with a few short portages around various falls. In the poorly drained Lowlands, the portages were rare. For four days, at one point, the scenery hardly changed. The Fawn kept winding back and forth through the spruce, and one little campsite looked like the previous one, though the usual Cree grave sites with their crosses or markers were each somewhat different. The last part of the Fawn and most of the lower Severn had several shootable limestone pitches.

Selections from our log follow:

> July 11, Day 3: (middle section only)
> … The marked rapid…flows around an "S" curve to the left and into a pond. In the last pitch stands a Gibraltar rock fairly close to the left shore. The last three ABS canoes—Mike well in the lead—successfully passed right of this rock (just under two metres tall above the water) using strong back ferries. Tom and Fred, in Tom's new Kevlar Old Town Canadienne did

Our campsite (l-r): Cathryn Rees, Michael Watts and Bruce Hodgins. Cree family graves marked with crosses can be seen in the background, up on a hill.

not. They broached classically, amidships tipping up-stream trapping some of the gear and spilling paddles, crew and the rest of the gear. The canoe flipped and buckled bottoms up to the thwarts, the great river flow pouring into the ends. It took about three hours to free the badly damaged boat. Using throw ropes, painters, several carabiners bound to tress, and several trips by canoe out to the rock to affix ropes, we finally pried it free. Bill's engineering skills were highly prized. Many of us had believed that the buckled Canadienne was finished, that we were now just after the gear. The bottom had two long rips, one lengthways and one crossways. Yet once free, it bounced back into shape. Parts of the thin outer layer of Kevlar was still intact. Still cold and some of us wet. Carol made a fire and cooked a very filling hot soup for lunch. We duct taped the wounds, and the boat floated.

July 22, Day 12: "Wapakopowastik or White Seal Rapids, the Day before Fort Severn"
Up at 7:00 a.m. Mike Watts was soloing and away at 8:15, the rest at 9:00. We were soon paddling against a light northern breeze. We noted a great deal of recent burn on the left bank, with a bit on the higher right bank. After catching up with Michael about 11:00, we landed on the left because we could hear the dull roar of Wapakopowistik Rapids. We cautiously approached a big limestone ridge or ledge on the left shore, as we could see the rapids begin on the right. The Severn was now well over a kilometre wide, all white below us, with the rapids especially high on the far side. The Rapids take place where the Severn goes around a major bend to the left, exposing the limestone ledges and breaks. Here is exposed a large, dry ledge area below the high riverbank, on the inside of this great curve.

We found the wide trail route across the point on the ledge, cutting the corner yet in sight of the River and rarely more than 150 metres from it. Much of the black spruce above the clay banks had been burned as had the undergrowth, all in 1994—no green yet reappearing.

These Rapids, the most northerly in Ontario, command great respect, and before shooting they should be very carefully examined. The drop must be over 10 metres along the Rapids' one kilometre course. There are several ledges. Our run was as close as possible to the left shore, but the ledges frequently require adventurous moves toward the very big stuff, at least 50 metres off shore. The bottom is very complex, with exposed, low limestone islands, reefs, jagged points and small bays. It is, however, all quite visible, with the steepest pitches near to the top. We first all carried a heavy load of gear over the portage and worked back along the shore, examining the route carefully. Bruce and Carol, Bill and Cathryn, and Mike shot down the full route, in about twelve minutes each, unscathed and with little water taken in. We did a lot of ferrying and a couple of high braces into eddies. Fred and Tom portaged the wounded Kevlar. We would not advise shooting loaded at any time. Full manoeuvrability is necessary. The Class is 3 ½, because it is so long and so complex. Yet the big holes and big waves were further to the right and not a problem; they could be very serious in higher water.

We lunched near the bottom end, amid flies; we noted some 1993 graffiti. Although we felt the north wind picking up, we recommenced our paddling, with Mike requiring lots of effort. Rounding the big bend to the east, we camped well before the first marked island, on the left bank amid a very spacious broken limestone-gravel verge, with patches of ground and fireweed before the true bank. It was truly a lovely if very alien environment. It was cool, with no bugs or flies, as the north wind continued.

After a rest we cooked up a dinner of salmon-vegetable quiche and re-hydrated beets. Morale was very high. Bed about 10:00 p.m.

During our stay at Fort Severn, William Koostachia, a Cree fisherman took us out in an outboard along the Hudson Bay coast. He "picked fish" out of his nets, which he walked to in low tide. Further out we almost frolicked from the outboard with six beluga whales." It was a totally captivating experience.

July 24, Day 14
... After resting, we walked about Fort Severn visiting various sites. We talked with the MNR fire-fighting manager; only the village and airport are protected

from fire. One fire was very close then, to the airstrip. We fried up fish we had been given and cooked up a macaroni dish.

That evening we visited (an invitation through Cathryn and Bill) the Health Centre [where they had been earlier]. We were hosted by Bernice, (the Cree who was the

A Cree fisherman, William Koostachia, checking his fish nets at low tide.

Professional Director), and her retired husband Bill Matthews. We had showers and there was lots of talk. One Cree woman, Marjorie K visited us and sold some handicrafts. Some [of our group] also found Jennifer, another Cree famous for her leather gloves and other crafts. Most walked to our campsite in the dark; Carol and Bruce were picked up by two young persons on an ATV and driven back.

The broad lower reaches of the Severn River are certainly very far to the north for Ontario. Remote Fort Severn situated above 56° North is the province's most northerly community. The many small Cree children were extremely friendly. Everywhere we went we were made to feel truly welcome. We enjoyed our visit, but we worried about Fort Severn's future; it was so isolated.

# 30

## THE NEARBY LADY EVELYN RIVER, TEMAGAMI, AND THE DISTANT MOUNTAIN RIVER, NORTHWEST TERRITORIES, 1995

In July, Bruce, Julie Sunday and Andrew Ouchterlony led a fly-in trip to Macpherson Lake, paddling downstream on the Lady Evelyn River to Wakimika Lake and Creek, and Obabika Lake to the northern part of Lake Temagami. This was in part to instruct and test some teachers from Crestwood Secondary School in Peterborough for their Ontario Recreational Canoeing Association Canoe Tripping certification. The teachers included: Robin Maughan, Marion McDougall, Jim Mulder, Larry Pearson and Cathy Symons. Others on the trip included: Kerry Cannon, Dawn and Kate Jamieson, Luella Nagy, Natalie Pearson and Dr. Brian Pell. The route included a side trip to Dry Lake and its Ridge, then on the North Branch of the Lady Evelyn and into Willow Island Lake and on to Diamond. From there, they paddled and portaged west into the Wakimika and Obabika rivers, then east and north into Temagami and back to Camp Wanapitei.

The trip required an air evacuation of Luella who was suffering from severe abdominal pain. This necessitated a single canoe on a very fast emergency express run, half of it in darkness, by Julie and Andrew from Bridal Veil Falls, back to Wanapitei and use of the camp phone. Luella was carried in a canoe as a mojo (a third person sitting in the middle of a canoe) to Willow Island Lake where a plane could land. With support, Luella was able to walk the portages. The plane picked up Andrew and Julia and brought them back to the group; it then flew Luella, accompanied by Brian, to the Sudbury Hospital where she spent several days before being released.

What follows is from the log of Day 3 beginning before Luella took sick:

> July 12, Day 3: "Dry Lake Ridge and Divide Lake"
> Up by 7:00, away from the Shangra-La site at 9:30 a.m. after a gala breakfast. After shooting a class 1½ set and entering Divide or Katherine Lake, we turned right and landed at the tiny outlet from Dry Lake. We carried four canoes (two Kevlars, two ABS) up the very rough trail to Dry Lake—"To hell and back," Kerry Cannon said.
>
> The trail begins to the left of the creek mouth and was very dense and much worse than Bruce remembered it from 1989. Few seem now to go to Dry Lake. More than half the way up, one must climb a granite knoll that leads off left, then descend steeply down to the shallow creek, walk across it and through marsh to the very shallow, clear but dense, weedy and muddy Dry Lake. We now had a clear sky and very hot temperature perhaps 40° C. We heard later that people were dying in Chicago.
>
> Landing at the small campsite at the southwest side and consuming lots of liquids and gorp, we headed into the bush toward the summit of the Dry Lake Ridge. We lost the disappearing trail very soon, amid lots of windfall. Soon we were climbing steeply, and many became quite tired. Fluids were essential. We found the rock section well to the south, but undoubtedly not far enough south for the 1989 climb or descent. Climbing upward on the rock cliffs, we did get good views of the Old Growth Forest. We had lunch at split levels. Robin demonstrated his compass skills. He climbed on to the south summit and then returned with information; he then started down with Kerry

and Luella (who was having grave difficulties with breath and a very fast [180] heartbeat). Others climbed higher and most made it to the summit—but not around the 360 degree circle (going west and north) as in 1989. Natalie Pearson was a great climber and was, perhaps, the youngest person ever to reach the summit of Dry Lake Ridge.

The route down was easier at first but then quite difficult, along the swamps and muddy bay back to the starting point. We were thirsty, despite the water bottles. We paddled in the heat and our fatigue, passed a "loon-at-rest," and then carried down over the portage.

Many swam right there, from shore or from the canoes, to cool off. Larry fed us power bars, which gave us energy to continue. Luella was not well. We paddled out onto Katherine (Divide) to the Narrows and camped on the spacious north (river left) side. Wonderful stove-prepared dinner of fettuccine, crab and chocolate fondue. The sky became overcast, and we had very light rain. The group was in a tired but buoyant mood, with a great sense of accomplishment. Some disliked the snakes at the site; others revelled in their presence. Some went to bed early, while Kerry and Natalie led others in games such as "The Moon is Round."

The trip had been great fun, despite the tension of Luella's evacuation and had been a learning experience for both the ORCA candidates and even the leaders, who were already certified. Larry Pearson obtained his Instructor's level in Canoe Tripping. By this time, certification at various levels had become a principal requirement for school-sponsored canoe-trip leadership.

Later that summer of 1995, in early August, ten of us tripped the Mountain River in the Northwest Territories. It would be Wanapitei's fifth trip on that most challenging and spectacular route.[8] We flew into Willow Handle Lake, one of the headwaters of the Mountain River at approximately 1,130 metres, in two twin Otter flights from Norman Wells, located on the lower Mackenzie River. Our route took us through the mountains, in most glorious weather and with spectacular, breathtaking views of the mountains, often in passes between giant rock cliffs.

"Well," said Bill Cormode on landing, "I guess that's all you can expect for a thousand dollar flight." Cathryn Rees, Barry Diceman, Dave Goslin, Don and Lynda Mason, Jack and Leila Nessen were on the trip.

We immediately set up camp in a cramped, previously used site. In the site fire pit we found, in a plastic jar under a rock, a note from Max Finkelstein of the Canadian Heritage Rivers System (and an Ottawa author[9]) wishing Bruce, Carol and the gang a great trip. He was running a couple of weeks ahead of us. We left a note for Jennifer Buck (ex-Wanapitei) who would be following us in a day or so leading a Trailhead/Black Feather group down the River.

From Willow Handle Lake we portaged, slightly over a kilometre, mainly through open tundra, to the tiny and shallow Push-Pull Creek, where we began our real paddling. This took us into a larger creek usually called Arctic Sky. Many caribou were milling about the stream's valley. We followed Arctic Sky, with great adventures and many animal sightings as described in our log (see below), onto the Mountain River itself.[10] We continued down the Mountain, through the mountains themselves, past the Moonscape and Tufa Mounds, the valley's warm and hot springs and then through the four canyons.

From the log, Days 8 and 9:

Carol and Bruce shooting rapids at the entrance to the first canyon. *Photo by Don Mason.*

## August 6, Day 8: "To the Moonscape and the Tufa Mounds"

Up at 7:00 am to see frost on the canoe bottom. Cool but warming fast....We were off at 10:15 to see fantastic changeable scenery, as the River braided even more, with long curves through a wide valley, fast water and lots of gravel bars. The majestic mountain formations varied greatly in colour, shape and even in types of rocks. On more than one occasion a part of the valley would be lower than our river course—very strange. We suddenly saw, before noon, several orange ribbons (as an alarm) on a huge gravel bar on river left. We stopped and carefully examined the bar and the river ahead. Finally we deduced that the ribbons marked the edges of a rough airstrip for a plane to land. Mystifying! We lunched on the bar and using the timer and Barry's tri-pod we took group photos, Carol often had the feeling of being in a fairyland, in a large bowl completely surrounded for 360° by the splendour of the mountains.

In the afternoon it was as if we were paddling down a water hill, so visibly steep was our swift descent. Very hot. We reached the great Moonscape on River left by a great bend in the River. We took at least an hour to hike up onto this huge bizarre, angled plateau and knoll; "the Moonscape" was probably created by an ancient and massive rock slide or perhaps it resulted from either some meteorite impact or a volcanic eruption. Totally fascinating and very different from anything else around, it was of various colours of beiges and yellow and different textures. The surrounding rock is mostly dislodged shale or ash, with here and there, moss and little bushes pushing through. There is one large cat-like statuesque remnant and several smaller ones standing up above the rubble, by a dry pond by tiny willows.

Then it was back in the canoes for our six-mile paddle to our anticipated campsite; the rocks in midstream became more numerous. Jack and Leila briefly let down their guard and attention and hit one of the rocks and over went the canoe. With help from Don and Lynda, they quickly got themselves and the canoe to river right. Jack was able to tell us that the thermarest (his make-do life jacket) worked as a PFD.[11]

We were looking for the "spring site," as noted in Shawn's 1994 trip report, and in one kilometre reached the site of the Tufa Mound Springs, just past the mouth of a creek on river right.

Following a dinner of a fusella pesto and date squares for dessert, we hiked up these amazing formations with their calcium deposits. There is a short steep route and a much longer one, a gentler climb on the downstream side. On top there are two small geysers gushing mineral water and there are several other calcium springs. Carol, Bill and Don hiked up much further past several more springs. Great views down the valley. We returned in time to watch a large

caribou buck cross the river. Warm evening. Bed
about 10:30 p.m. Cooled down at night.

August 11, Day 9: "Second Canyon and the R3s"
Up at 7:15 to clear sky. Breakfast—hot peanut cereal
followed by sautéed veggie tofu mix. Away at 10:15
into the approaches to the Second Canyon. The
entrance was tricky with our high water, as a big boil
and wave on the right came before Battleship Rock.
The route must be bent left, while paddling in a turn
closely following river left, watching out for right
side gravel bars. Then we swung left because in 400
metres came the bigger problem. The river curves
and then turns left; this side must be hugged, but
only gently to avoid the gravel. Suddenly we were
into a powerful eddy, which twirled us around. Yet
the build-up on river right was huge and ominous.
So we paddled "up" the eddy, which is down the
river, and re-entered the main current through
a narrow gap between surface rocks. While in the
eddy, this was first checked from the left shore, the
run was not too hard. Below, the route was easy and
very beautiful.

Paddling on, we stopped on river left, just after
the Stone Knife River entered on that side; much
clearer (turquoise) than the upper Mountain,
it seemed almost as large. The waves were now
consistently big, as we passed Shawn Hodgins' 1994
campsite on the right. Soon we came to what Shawn
had identified as a very "Wavy Class II Rapids."
We, in this high water, would call it at least Class
III, perhaps more. Landing on a huge gravel bar
to our right, in river centre, we found ourselves by
the larger ("A" water) of three channels. Pictures of
others running the set were taken, some from the top
and some from the bottom of the rapids. Carol and

Bruce ran on the right side of the "A" water, passing the entry on the right of the small "B" water and the medium size "C" water. We were thus somewhat to the right of the largest waves, but still it was a great roller coaster.

We lunched on the continuation of the gravel bar. We soon entered the Half Canyon with its huge cliffs along the left side, which curves to the right. There were high waves and shoals in the approach, but none running fairly close to the cliff walls. Then we came to a big rock pile point on the left where Shawn had alerted us about a "R3 Chute." We walked this huge bar, passed an R2 and could see the gravel island downstream and the small left channel which avoided fairly large waves in the right channel. So we took this left channel, but nothing looked as daunting as our previous so-called "wavy R2." How the River can change!

It was then almost continuous R2s while we experienced very hot clear weather, tiring us very considerably. Some were even cranky as we looked for a suitable campsite. Finally we found one, on river left, a few kilometres onto the 106H2 map at GR 072123. It was great, though we had to make a tricky fast landing with no eddy. Thunder storms and black clouds rolled around us, from both sides and from down the valley, heavy wind gusts but no rain.

Smoked oysters and crackers, then a dinner of sukiyaki, rice, cabbage salad with mandarin oranges, lots and lots of fruit juice, Gatorade, dessert of dried fruit and Dave's Quaker Oats granola bars. Good morale now, with lots of chatter and the reading of the trip log of Wanapitei's Voyageur IIs (led by Andrea Hodgins and Mike Craig in 1993) similar day. Temperature today reached 25°C in the sun. Bed around 10:00 p.m. Still light enough to read inside the tent at 11:00 p.m.

Relaxing on the lower Mountain River (l-r): Leila Nessen, Don Mason, Barry Diceman and Bill Cormode.

Then it was on through fast current and waves through the third and fourth canyon and finally into the lowlands as we approached the Mackenzie River. We had paddled about three hundred kilometres, and for most of it you could feel and see that you were going downhill. There was only the one portage that did not involve a drop, at the beginning into the creek, and there were no falls on the River.

At the mouth of the Mountain River we camped for the night and early the next afternoon Frank Pope with two Dene helpers arrived from Norman Wells with three outboard motor boats. Our rough, cold trip upstream on the Mackenzie River to Norman Wells took just over four hours. At the hotel that night we had hot showers, and celebrated with a wonderful dinner. The following day we flew home.

Is it not strange that the great canyons number upstream on the south on the Nahanni River and downstream on the Mountain River? The answer, of course, is that Euro-Canadians explored the South Nahanni working upstream early in the twentieth century and explored the Mountain much later, beginning in 1972; the latter flew in, either from the Yukon or Norman Wells and paddled downstream.[12] The Dene, of course, had been there long before, but very few of their place names survive.

# 31

## THE UPPER STURGEON RIVER AND
## BACK TO THE SOPER, BAFFIN ISLAND, 1996

Bruce and Carol, plus Larry Pearson, led another ORCA training trip in July, consisting mainly of Peterborough teachers and spouses, including Robin and Rosemary Maughan, Bob and Mary McLaughlin, Vaughan McMillan, Andrea Lea, Jim Mulder, Sharon Pearson, John Reid, Steve Reynolds and Leslie Warren. We flew west from Wanapitei into Scarecrow Lake, climbed Ishpatina Ridge to the Tower (an old abandoned fire tower) in the mist and rain, and continued southwest through Hamlow Lake and down Stull Creek out onto the upper Sturgeon River.

Our log records a description:

> July 14, Day 2: "Ishpatina Ridge and Stull Creek"
> Bob, Larry and Robin were up at 6:30 to start the fire. Had breakfast at 7:30 a.m. (bacon, eggs, muffins, oatmeal and coffee). Sharon led a discussion on kitchen and meal organization.
>
> Robin led us on a very organized hike up the Ishpatina Ridge (highest point in Ontario [692 metres]). We left at 9:30 a.m. and hiked for about 1¾ hours in the rain. We arrived at the summit at approx. 11:15. Unfortunately there was no view, due to the misty weather. There were large trees (white pine approx. 200–300 years old) and interesting fauna and flora (pitcher plant). There were

lots of moose droppings along the trail. We all stopped at the big white pine to hug it and have our picture taken (group shot). It took about 1½ hours to hike down.

We paddled back to our campsite on the island and enjoyed a nice lunch (tortillas with salsa, tomatoes, cucumbers, kolbasa and oranges). The sun came out and it was a beautiful day. We decided as a group to pack up and head for the next campsite. We were all packed to leave at 4:00 p.m.

It was supposed to be a 3 hr. trip from what we had been told. We expected to arrive in our next campsite around 7:30 p.m.

We talked to Erin, staff from Camp Northwaters on Hamlow Lake at 6:30, and she predicted it would take 1½ hours to get to our campsite down Stull Creek. The weather was still beautiful.

We arrived at Stull Creek around 7:00 p.m. Our first obstacle was a log jam. (Hap Wilson's log of

Kandi, Carol and Bruce's dog, in her pink lifejacket, in a canoe being lined down Stull Creek.

Stull Creek does not do justice to the difficulty of the creek.)

We ran into more obstacles. In "Rocky Rapids" (sect. 5 in Hap's report)[13] there was no portage, so the group had to line the canoes. It was the first time lining for some of the group, and they all did an excellent job. Steve and Jim were a big help—thanks! (We also had a carry over with full canoes—WOW!) The portages we encountered were treacherous due to very wet conditions. Larry had to go downstream and cut a couple of trees and some branches to clear a route for us to get through. We entered a swift and saw a canoe on the left shore that had been smashed up. It was now 9:30 and we pressed on. We went through some cedars, then some swifts, and ended up in sections 6 & 7 (of Hap's map) where we had to line and carry canoes over a 3 ft. drop, ending up at a log jam to the left and a shallow rocky path to our right.

It was now 10:00 p.m. and beginning to get dark. It was too late to attempt any more barriers, and we were all too tired. The group decided to camp. There were no possible sites on the right shore, as it was all boulders. Using a flashlight Sharon found some possible sites on the left shore in the woods. It was suggested that people double up in tents (couples) as there was limited space. Vaughan and Andrea decided to sleep under the stars (there were lots of bugs). Everyone handled the situation really well. Although we had a number of falls during the day while lining and on portages, no one was seriously hurt (Rosemary sprained her ankle). While people put up tents and got organized, Jim made hot chocolate on his stove and we had some bagels and cream cheese. It sure hit the spot after an exhausting day! We headed off to bed around midnight. It was a beautiful starry night.[14]

We followed the Sturgeon for three-and-a-half days to and then up the Obabika Creek and Lake. Amid high wind and rain and with delays, we paddled back to Wanapitei. A second Wanapitei adult group (non-ORCA) was running close behind us, one that included Myk and Doreen Bartlett who had longed tripped with us. They did not take the Stull Creek route but instead portaged along a partly overgrown former logging road for several kilometres across to the Sturgeon River. Both groups paddled together into camp.

ORCA certification was and is especially important for secondary school teachers taking students on canoe-tripping excursions. Larry Pearson was a director of the outdoor experiential education program at Crestwood Secondary School in Peterborough. Like ourselves (Bruce and Carol), Larry had his ORCA instructor's certification in canoe tripping as well as considerable standing in moving water and lake water. The course presented on this trip brought most of the participants up to a certification skill level. All the candidates were experienced paddlers and did very well. We also had lots of fun and lots of laughter and morale was very high even in the midst of Stull

Creek. The route is especially beautiful, typical Temagami country with all its variations, old growth red and white pine, rugged granite ridges, small meandering creeks, the swift Sturgeon River, waterfalls and small clear lakes. The fact that we climbed up to the highest point in Ontario on Ispatina Ridge was a bonus.

Larry and Sharon Pearson.

In August 1996 we (Carol and Bruce) led our second trip on the Soper River, taking us back again to Baffin Island. (For route details see the 1993 account.) This group involved Kerry Cannon, Cathy and Jim Davison, Daryl Hodgins, Solomon and Daniel Minkin, Linda and Bob Rodney, Tom Romans, Bernice and Dale Standen and Bev Haun. The Soper, or Kuujuaq, flows through, what had recently become the Katannilik, "the place of the waterfalls," Territorial Park, a park (1500 sq. km) in the southeast part of Baffin Island. The beautiful Soper Valley runs through the centre of the Park.

> August 8, Day 2: "Hiking Up Mount Joy"
> Tom was up before six and walked the small plateau above and behind the tents. Daniel was up when Carol got out of her tent at 6:30. Granola, boiled eggs, bacon, bread with PB, honey or jam for breakfast. Out of 14 there were only 6 coffee drinkers. We also had beverage crystals of various flavours, herbal and black tea and hot chocolate and the water was drinkable without purifying it.
>
> We left the campsite at 9:30 and walked to the River's edge. Since we had some inexperienced canoeists Bruce had a lesson on ferrying before we paddled across the River to begin our day hike up Mount Joy, directly across from our first campsite. We began our ascent at 10:10. Some had more rests than others as we hiked up, arriving at the small lake near the summit at 12:15 p.m. where we lunched in the sunshine and light breeze. It was very pleasant. Lunch of crackers and pita bread with cream cheese with Robin Young's scrumptious blueberry-elderberry jam

(made back at camp the day we left) on top. Snacked on granola bars.

Daniel and Solomon then hiked around the lake counter-clockwise. Bev, Tom, Cathy, Jim and Carol climbed up the last hill of the Mount behind our lunch spot. Others took shorter hikes and relaxed by the lake. We then met up and started hiking along the top of the ridge. After a short distance Daryl Hodgins, the Standens and Daniel began their descent and the rest of us continued on the ridge until we reached the Inukshuk at the southern end, at which point we could look down at the confluence of the Soper and Joy rivers below, and the Soper Valley beyond. We also had quite a panoramic view of the area. Although it is very barren in a rugged sense, the deep valley of the Soper River is very lush with lichens, ferns, grasses, club-mosses and beautiful wildflowers, and in some gullies small willow bushes are found. In one area are found willow trees up to about 3 metres in height. Started back at 3:45 p.m. Part of the actual descent after we left the plateau was rather difficult. The rocky terrain was a challenge for Kerry Cannon. She survived better than her treasured boots, held together by duct tape. It was a great day. About 12 caribou were sighted; one came to within about 8 m. of Bob Rodney who did not have his camera.

Dinner—mulligatawny stew with added broccoli, parsnips and dumplings. We baked brownies with our smaller (7" diameter) new Dutch oven. They were a great success. The evening had a red sunset go down over the hill behind us. Bed at 9:30 p.m.

Although this was our second Arctic trip on the Soper River, the group, the warm weather and the water levels were so different that it seemed almost like a first descent. The Soper is such a wonderful river and we had such a welcoming stay at the end in Kimmirut (the name meaning "heal" in Inuktituk.) For our cruise in three power boats down the fjord at the end of our trip, out into Hudson Strait, we now were obliged to wear bright orange survival suits. The sea was calm and the sun was shining and we watched the seals bobbing about near numerous icebergs. The next day we flew to Iqaluit and then back to Ottawa. Carol and Bruce would be back again in 2001.

# 32

## PADDLING IN THE EVERGLADES AND IN BAJA: BACK TO THE THELON, 1997

This time we had a third leader, Jeff Edwards, who worked out the logistics for this particular voyage. He drove the Camp van and all of the canoes to Florida and back, a great help on our February canoe trip. We, along with all the participants flew south, some to Miami and some to Fort Lauderdale. Jeff met us at the airports and then drove us in the van to Everglade City. Participants included Molly Blyth, John Milloy, a Trent colleague, John Scott, a Wanapitei trip leader in the 1960s, Clair Rannie, also former camp staff, Lynn Stockfish, Berva MacDonald, Jean and Ralph Pope.

Basically we paddled out through channels to the Keys, then southeast through various mangrove islands and wide channels, and across sand bars, finally heading up one of the Turner "River canals," in a very narrow overhung passage, to the highway. We camped on beaches of beautiful keys on constructed chichees (platforms) set among the mangrove keys. The ones here were packed with mangrove trees, but some, however, had lovely sandy beaches which we could lunch or camp on.

What follows are various sections from Carol's seven-day trip report, which was written up during the trip:

> From Day 1: We easily found the West Pass, a long channel of only a few hundred metres in width. We began to see lots of birds, ibis, pelicans and osprey. We were protected from the wind in the pass, but for the

last nautical 1¼ miles we were going against heavy headwinds. At one point we heard a shriek behind us coming from Lynn and Berva, as "something" knocked the back of their canoe. As we were nearing Tiger Key, our destination for the night, suddenly the Pope canoe took quite a lurch and part of a large back belonging to a manatee (sometimes referred to as a sea-cow) came out of the water having gone under their canoe. That "something" already mentioned was also a manatee... Luckily no canoe was tipped.

From Day 2: Continuing on we soon landed at a beach on the extreme west end of a point of Jewel Key. We were sheltered somewhat by the islands as we paddled this last stretch, but for the last couple of hundred metres we again met heavy headwinds. It was now 3:30 p.m. and we were too tired, and it was too far to paddle on to Rabbit Key, so we set up camp in among the mangroves. Several people walked part way around the island but Jeff, Jean, Ralph and I (Carol) walked around the whole key—through the mangroves, across little sandy beaches and in water over dead coral and through some muck.

The temperature was in the high 70s F (mid-20s C), and it was warm and sunny with clouds. By dinner the temperature dropped about 5°. Jeff provided another delicious meal, fresh veggies— cauliflower, potatoes, carrots, etc. with lentils, and rice, preceded by crackers and cheese. Relaxed evening. Wind went from heavy to light to heavy but never let up, and it swung 180°. Because of the wind we were lucky and had no bugs, nor did we have any raccoons, although footprints and one or two beasts were spotted. We were told they could be quite aggressive, particularly at Picnic and Tiger

Keys. To be raccoon proof, we hung our garbage pack and our barrels and two coolers.

From Day 4: Following our lunch break we continued paddling SE and then south until we reached Mormon Key with its long sandy beach. It was very appealing and since it was 2:30 p.m. we decided to stay. We were scheduled to go about another three miles [5 km metric] to New Turkey Key, but decided that since we were encountering such heavy winds and would have to retrace our "steps" the next day we would now stop. We took a short walk down the beach and decided where we would camp and then we all went for a delightful swim. The water, warmer than the previous day... As darkness approached Lynn and Berva decided to go and unpack in their tent, then we heard a scream. While changing Berva found a very much alive scorpion on her thigh. Their flashlights were in the tent, so Bruce went and got his light and they literally tore the tent apart to be sure there were no other undesirable creatures within. Fortunately it was removed without biting... [In unknown territory, always close the zippers after putting up a tent.]

From Day 5: About one mile before Watson Place, a tiny abandoned settlement, we met the park ranger who stopped for a chat. A second person with her was a volunteer worker, also female. The latter was from "The Beach" in Toronto and was a recent 4th year graduate from U. of Guelph. She was doing research and tracking manatee (which had been banded). After chatting a bit and being given some information we waved goodbye and continued up river, against the wind but with the tide, the latter being slightly stronger.

Soon afterwards the ranger returned and again chatted with Jeff... The ranger, with handcuffs jangling from one side of her belt and a revolver on the other, jokingly (with a straight face) told Jeff she might put her silver bracelets on him for camping "illegally" the night before (Mormon Key instead of Turkey Key). With his adrenaline running high, he politely told her he was more frightened by the hardware on the other side of her belt. She told him some folklore about Watson Place and then by phone with park headquarters, she changed our day's destination to the Sweetwater chickee. [These wooden platform on stilts, with two large areas separated by a narrow section with a portable toilet, provide the only place to camp in the interior part of the mangrove swamps.] The mosquito population at Watson Place was formidable as this year's rains and winds had been much heavier than usual.)

Jeff was given a ribbing for "hitching" a ride

alongside the ranger's boat to catch up to us... Continuing up the Chatham River we took the right channel past a very large island and then went to the right of the next island... We continued heading northeast, crossed a main boat channel, and took the middle course of three

Molly Blyth and Clair Rannie preparing lunch on the chickee in the Everglades.

choices … We then found the very narrow long channel into Sweetwater Bay, and after about ½ mile we crossed the bottom of the bay and went north up a long narrow channel for another ½ mile and here we found Sweetwater Chickee on the left behind a tiny island. We arrived at our Sweetwater at 1:45 p.m., lunched on gado gado perched on our chickee in a pleasant breeze.

While others relaxed, Jeff, Bruce and Carol went for an hour's paddle wandering through smaller channels of the mangroves ("womangroves" according to Jeff). While we were away Berva, being confined on the small chickee, took a tumble into the canoe and from there into the water. Fortunately, she was not hurt, but the glass Coleman globe was destroyed.

From Day 6: About two-thirds of the way down, still following the markers, we found #123 on a point on our left (west) mainland shore. Almost directly opposite this marker and only a smidgen to the west I (Carol) spied what I thought looked like a small opening. We investigated and found "OUR" Sunday chickee Bay tucked in behind two islands on the NE side of Sunday Bay and hidden from the main channel.

Lunched on left over rice, hummus and crackers, cheese, lettuce, celery and carrot sticks with lemonade. Lazed about on the double chickee (each about 10" x 10" with a 20" x 4" walk between them with a honey bucket behind the middle of the walkway) with nowhere to go. Bruce and John Milloy served tea. It was extremely tough on John because we only had brown sugar and he only likes white. He begrudgingly satisfied his sweet tooth with honey. Fortunately we had lots of "proper" tea for him along with the herbal.

Jeff made brownies on the outback oven, but we decided to enjoy them as dessert with our dinner of crab fettuccini. We also nibbled on hummus and crackers. We decided to put up tents. It was somewhat of a struggle, space wise. We finished cleanup just as darkness descended. Lynn and Berva went into their tent and could be heard laughing and chatting. Bruce and Jeff went solo for moonlight paddles, and the rest of us dangled our legs over the connecting link between the two chickees, the latter filled up with tents. Another beautiful moonlight night. At 7:30 p.m. we thought it was about midnight—such is life in the land of no twilight….

From Day 7: They told us it was possible if one went slowly to take a small motor boat up the Turner to the highway. They better not try it! Most of the boats we met appeared very macho, fast, high riding and usually occupied by two males.

To begin with, the Turner River was about 50 metres. As we went up the river, where it split, we took two left turns and one right turn. We entered an area of sawgrass area often referred to as Everglades river grass, and scattered palm trees began to appear. When we came to a three-way split, all narrow, we took the middle (straight ahead) channel. The right led to the canal, which further up has been permanently blocked off. For the first time we met numerous canoeists out on day trips, and one motorized canoe as well as two small motor boats. The river continued to get narrower, and we went through about three ponds.

We had a floating lunch and then, being six canoes huddled together crossways, stayed in a very narrow section. We had to let our canoes separate when a motor boat wanted through. Between a couple of ponds we went through a "mangrove tunnel" as the river was less than a canoe length in width and we were engulfed in mango branches. We had to push and pull our way through; another small pond and then a continuation of the small roofed-over tunnel, only this time the water became so shallow we had to literally pole our way through. John (JDS) and Claire tested the bottom and found it to be stable, so they got out of their canoe and pulled and pushed. Claire wasn't too happy because she kept wondering what there might be in the murky water that might attack. Molly thought she was Tarzan or Jane and helped pull their canoe standing up and pulling on the overhead branches (it worked). It was hard work. Navigationally we felt we were on the correct channel, but at times we wondered; we did see some sawed-off branches. Finally we came to a widening in the river which was very weedy; and then we met a kayaker, so we knew we were in the right place. The kayaker soon had to turn back as there was no way he could get through using his long paddle. In the last kilometre we began to see our first alligators, about six baby ones; but no doubt mother was close by. We soon pulled out at a bridge over the highway.

This was a marvellous experience with a fun-loving group. We, who were used to camping in the Far North, now had to be careful about alligators, not bears. Being much closer to the equator we had about the same amount of darkness as light and much of the interesting fauna and flowers were different. We didn't know what a manatee was until we "met up" with two of them. We much preferred experiencing some of old Florida, rather than basking on its crowded beaches.

Our next 1997 adventure took us to Mexico. This was our first of three wonderful coastal sea kayaking trips along the coast, in among the islands of the Sea of Cortez, off the Town of Loreto. Wanapitei (first the camp and then C.A.N.O.E.) has been doing these Baja trips most winters since this one, always under Shawn Hodgins' direction. This one, taken in March 1997, was Wanapitei's first: Shawn was with us, and in charge. We put in at Loreto, paddled north, just offshore, then crossed over to Isla Coronadas. We camped about two kilometres further eastward at a glorious spot in a sheltered bay.

The next morning we made the crossing from Isla Coronadas to Isla el Carmen, the largest and longest of the islands. This crossing was about eighteen kilometres, and the sea was calm. It took us about three hours. From here we paddled south and along the inside shore by beautiful bays, shoals, beaches and rock formations, all under a clear blue sky. We camped at Puerto Ballandra, a wonderful wilderness site with great both short and long hiking opportunities, up the dry arroyo. From there we paddled, hiked and camped along the west coast of El Carmen, the Island. We then paddled south over to the east side of the Isla Danzante following its nooks and crannies to the shore of its long southern beach. After camping overnight, we crossed back to the mainland at Escondido for our pick-up and return north to Loreto.

We enjoyed the small town of Loreto, dining, walking and visiting historic buildings, especially the Jesuit church built back in the Spanish era when Loreto was the capitol of California. The Jesuits had arrived in 1697.

Out on the waters and on the scenic beaches the group was alone and we revelled in the usually clear blue skies, the warm and even hot days and the cooler nights. We will go back.

Bruce and Carol kayaking in Baja. *Photo by Shawn Hodgins.*

The year 1997 was a very active year for paddling. August found both of us, Carol and Bruce embarking on our second trip on the Thelon River, at that time in a section of the Northwest Territories that is now Nunavut. This time we flew in and out from Baker Lake—probably a mistake. We were to be put down on the tundra as close as possible to the junction of the Hanbury and the upper Thelon rivers. On our first 1981 trip the plane from Yellowknife had been on floats. This time the plane had tires. Due to aircraft problems with our planned flight with Ptarmigan Airways, and after a three-day delay, we were able to get a Calm Air plane to come from Thompson, Manitoba, to fly us in to the River.

We "walked" and paddled down the last sixty or so kilometres of the upper Thelon to the forks (merger) with the Hanbury and on down to Beverly Lake. Jon and Shelagh Grant flew in to join us for the second half of the trip. We saw caribou, muskox and wolverine, sik-siks, (an Arctic ground squirrel), eagles, falcons, etc., but not as many as in 1981. Given our delays at the beginning, the trip became rather rushed.

The log excerpts that follow were written by Carol for publication in *Nastawgan,* the journal published by the Wilderness Canoeing Association:

> Friday 1, August:
> We took off at 8:35 a.m. The plane did not have large tundra tires; the young pilots were unfamiliar with the area and had never landed on the tundra before. They said we would be flying below the clouds...,
>
> About one half hour before landing, the plane began to do a lot of circling. The pilots borrowed *my* topo maps of the area including the junction of the two rivers and asked me where in relationship to the latter, had we put in on our 1981 trip....
>
> We did some more circling over a sandy esker and on the third approach made a good landing.
>
> We checked the co-ordinates of Don's [Mason] GPS with that of the plane, and the pilots said they were the same except that those given them by Ptarmigan were "over there a bit, over the middle of some water."
>
> The six of us [Bill Cormode, Don Mason, Phil Huggins, Fred Najork, Diana Paterson and I] were very apprehensive about our location. We estimated, by looking at both the map and the GPS, that we were 30 km upstream from the junction of the Hanbury and upper Thelon rivers. The plane was unloaded, including the fuel barrel that had been in front of my legs during the flight. The pilots were in a hurry to leave, being somewhat anxious about the take-off from the esker. They took my map with them to show Bruce and the rest of the group where we had been put down. We were upset about it, and we let the pilots know. They told us we were only about one kilometre from the river, which we could not see.

After they left we discussed our predicament and what our alternatives might be. We decided we would start the portage, realizing Bruce had one set of maps and the pilots had my topo map of the area. We set out with Don's GPS. After walking 1200 m and not even being able to see the river we realized we were not even half way. Some more scouting was done from different directions. Finally, Cathryn and Lynda found a spot on a nearby elevation from which they could see the river in the far distance.

We hoped that Bruce, upon seeing where we were, would have the pilots land his group downstream of the rivers' junction and then come and relocate us. This is exactly what Bruce tried to do when his flight left Baker Lake at 3:45 p.m. He emphasized the nature of the canyon with its big rapids to the pilots. He also stated that we had already lost three days of a very limited 15-day trip. He informed them that Boris Kotelewetz [agent] and Ptarmigan had assured him that there were many places to land downstream of the confluence, one within a couple of kilometres and, if that was not suitable, one within eight kilometres at Warden's Grove, where it was possible to land. He also discussed the 1978 Russian Cosmos discovery and the arrival of planes of many different sizes to help in the search and evacuation of the people living at Warden's Grove.[15] The pilots agreed they would try and land there, and then go and retrieve the rest of us.

They flew over Warden's Grove, and Bruce thought all was well when suddenly without comment they veered over the canyon and the rapids and then landed on the sandy esker with us. The pilots stipulated that there was no place to land at Warden's Grove. When asked about the cabins they said they were no longer there. (This was proven wrong several days later when we stopped and walked around the area.) Now the pilots asserted that they did not have enough fuel to move two plane loads from the esker to Warden's Grove. They then said the rapids did not look too big (they obviously were not canoeists). [The trip was not advertised as one with white-water and we had some participants not comfortable in more than light rapids].

This was all very strange when in Baker Lake it had been emphasized that with the low-water level there were more places than usual to land. Bruce asked whether this meant there was nothing more to discuss and the pilots replied there was not. The pilots asked if we could cope. Bruce replied we could with the gravest of difficulty, and we were very upset and unhappy....

From Cathryn Rees's journal: "Lynda [Mason] and I found a straight route 22 minutes long to the river from there. Ate at 11 p.m. All are very tired. I did a lot towards dinner and did the dishes. Was last one up.... later it was estimated the portage was five miles not kilometres."

Although all experienced canoeists, we were greatly concerned and had no idea what we would face on the long portages. Since there were no portages on our planned route, we had been assured beforehand that the pilots had the co-ordinates for landing from Ptarmigan Airways and that we would be put down within a few hundred metres of the river, the group had decided we did not need tumps and barrel-carrying straps, so we had left them in Baker Lake.

The average age was 57 years and some had problems not conducive to lengthy portaging and certainly were not prepared psychologically for it. [We had packed for a no-portaging trip]. As it turned out we had about ten kilometres to carry, including the initial one and then one around the canyon. Some had to portage three and even four times, in order to get all the "gear" across. Lynda, Cathryn, Don, Bill C, Fred and Phil all carried extra for Diana and Bill Paterson and me. They just kept going.

Lynda also always helped around the campfire and packed up the kitchen every morning. Cathryn did a lot of food preparation and dishwashing. Bruce did not need help, but had to admit that he is was no longer as fast as he once was. With the help from Don and Bill C. we had more than two leaders, and Don was also official photographer. The group was very supportive and stayed together. However, we were not without our tense times as all were "leaders." It certainly meant for some interesting dynamics.

While it had been cold in Baker Lake, on the esker (grid reference 018024 on the 1:250,000 map) here it was warm and sunny We portaged northwest across the tundra arriving at the side of a small lake with thousands of blackflies swarming in the low tundra vegetation. Although tired we paddled westward about 500 m to a more suitable camping spot. Cathryn and Lynda scouted out a route to the river while the rest of us set up camp. Bed around midnight after being up since 5:30 a.m. It had been a long and stressful day.[16]

We did get to the River and we did paddle to the top of the big rapids. The Thelon turns 90 degrees left, close to the bottom of the rapids. After serious scouting we decided to cross to the left bank and carry the canoes and gear about five kilometres, diagonally across the hypotenuse and then lower them down the high to the River. It was very hard. After that the morale did pick up and we had a great time paddling down past the junction with the Hanbury, down past Warden's Grove. We then missed the 1926–27 site where

John Hornby, his nephew and friend had wintered and starved to death. Jon and Shelagh joined us for the second week of the trip. We were all sitting in our canoes on the River, waving madly as they flew over us. They were much further up the River before the plane turned around, came back and found us.

Just before entering Beverly Lake, as we paddled by, we recognized our 1981 campsite on the left. At the entrance of the Lake on the river right we set up camp. After climbing up the rather steep bank onto the flat tundra, and putting down our packs we disturbed what seemed like thousands of blackflies. We cooked and ate on the beach in our bug tents. We did have many good times and saw quite a few animals, including a wolverine. We loved the area but with the problems at the beginning and the resulting necessary push, we did not have the time to relax or do the fishing as planned. As a result, the group never fully jelled. We were picked up by a Ptarmigan plane on wheels and flown back to Baker Lake in two loads.

# 33

## SEA KAYAKING IN BAJA AGAIN AND
## ON TO THREE MARITIME RIVERS, 1998

This our second winter kayaking trip to Baja had Lara Payne from Gabriola, the company that took canoes down to Baja in the winter time, as kayaking leader while we (Bruce and Carol) were the group leaders for Wanapitei C.A.N.O.E.  Besides the three of us, the group included Dave and Liz Ariano, Ivan Bateman, a long-time Peterborough and Wanapitei friend, and Jilian and Dick Scarth. The Scarths, now living in Vancouver, were old friends who used to canoe with us and our families when they lived in Peterborough.

On this trip we were taken by van up the coast of the Baja peninsula and into a beach at San Nicholas, a small bay within one hundred kilometres directly north of Loreto. We then spent six days winding our way back, paddling our kayak in and around numerous small bays until we reached the Bay of Ensenada San Juanico, where we were picked up and driven back to Loreto.

We had much heavier wind on this trip than on our previous one. We were only able to paddle a short distance the first day.  A trip the following day was windbound before we could even put paddles in the water. As we slowly, partly because of the wind, moved our way south we took time to walk on the beaches, swim and snorkel. Sometimes we would be stopped near an arroyo, a bolder-strewn dry streambed winding down out of the hills. There were lots of cactus trees to dodge around and the landscape was dotted with pretty, bright red, yellow and blue flowers and very interesting rock formations.  The wind would usually die down at night and then come up in the afternoon. Therefore, we would get up at 6:00 a.m. and then watch the sun rise just before 7:00 a.m. In the evenings we would sometimes star gaze and pick out various star constellations, Orion, Betelgeuse, Pleiades and Sirius. The moon arose around 1:00 a.m. and the Big Dipper was very low in the northern sky.

Carol wrote in her log:

Day 2, Feb 17:
Lara gave a wake-up call at 6:00 a.m. Liz and Dave were on for breakfast—muesli and delicious pancakes with real maple syrup and mandarin oranges. Getaway was at 8:45 a.m. We had been paddling about 10 minutes when Bruce heard a snap, and we were rudderless. Lara came alongside and said we were either without a rudder or it was under the water. Fortunately it was under the water, and the wires were still attached. She put the rudder in its deck-resting place. Since we had another point to get around and the wind was picking up, we opted to keep going; otherwise we feared we might not get around the point before the wind became too strong.

Because it was a long bay, instead of going diagonally out towards the point, we followed the arc of the shoreline to keep our options open. There was one more small beach which we could go into if necessary. However, we did get into the lee as we followed the shoreline out to the point. We did hit heavy wind as we went around the Punta Pulpito, and there were some small reefs to avoid. We moved ahead, and Lara kept with the group as we paddled into another lovely sandy beach on the other side of the point. We relaxed, took pictures and walked on the beach while Lara, Bruce and Ivan fixed the rudder. It was not an uncommon problem; the pin in the rudder dropped below the part it was attached to on the kayak. Due to the grinding of the sand the hole probably gradually deepened. Kayaks are very expensive, but the rudders certainly have a weakness.

Following the repair job we continued paddling close by the shore avoiding numerous reefs. The wind picked up and then dropped. It was very gusty which slowed our pace. There were many interesting rock formations to look at, and the scenery was absolutely magnificent. We stopped at 1:30 p.m. on a gravel beach with a step up to a small sandy area where four of the tents were put up. Lara put hers not too far away, but on the gravel at the base of a high cliff. On the map, about 300 metres north of our campsite, between it and Gull Rock, is marked a tidal hot springs at low tide. After the campsite marked on the map is the name Caleta Saquicismunde. Our campsite was at the mouth of a dry arroyo.

It was Ivan's lunch, and he cooked up a tasty meal of sliced potatoes and tuna in a cheese sauce with extra mozzarella and clams and served with a half an avocado and lime juice. We then relaxed, some swam, some walked, and some slept. We had dinner in the daylight at 6:45 p.m. After dinner a very light, short-lived sprinkle of rain fell, but we did put up our "sun" tarp and then sat around by candlelight while Dick and Liz played their harmonicas and Dick sang some old songs and tried to teach us Dona Nobis Pacem (Liz knew it). There were lots of stars in the sky, so some star gazing took place.

We loved being back in Baja. Although we love our winters we did enjoy the warmth. We had great fun and morale was high, even with the high wind that rose, especially in the afternoons. The winds meant we stopped earlier than sometimes planned but then had more time to hike in the countryside so different from ours, with its volcanic hills

Carol making pancakes on their second Baja kayaking trip. *Photo taken by Shawn Hodgins.*

The people in Loreto were friendly and we felt safe walking in the town; one could spend time in a store not being pressured to buy anything and we particularly enjoyed our special restaurant meal celebrating the last night. Loreto is blessed with pure drinking water from its deep artesian wells, which require no purification.

All three Maritime Rivers, the Shelburne in Nova Scotia, the Hillsborough in Prince Edward Island and the Maragee on Cape Breton Island in Nova Scotia, are rivers of the Canadian Heritage Rivers System. For this July trip some of our group drove to our rallying point, and some were already in the Maritimes; most met at the home of John and Mary Scott in Sandy Cove, Nova Scotia. We (Bruce and Carol) first co-led a trip with John in 1959, and have remained friends since then. Included in the group were the Pearsons, (Larry, Sharon, Natalie, Emily and Dustin). Anna Marie Kelly and Alan Law joined us for the latter two rivers. Meaghan McLaren drove from Ontario with the Pearsons and the Hodginses, but she suddenly left the trip, after the first day on the Hillsborough River.

We put in at Jake's Landing in Kejimkujik National Park, onto the estuary of the upper Mersey River and paddled across Keji Lake. From there we portaged and entered some other small lakes, linked by more portages, until we reached Stillwater Lake on the upper Shelburne River in the centre of the southern part of the Nova Scotia Peninsula. We paddled down the Shelburne to the Mersey River, a journey of five days.

It was a wonderful wilderness voyage with good scenery, mostly light rapids, along with a few short portages. We did, however, have some lining in a shallow rocky area of the River. Under sail, we moved along the north shore of Rossignol Lake to the take-out place.

Two days were spent on the south "flowing" Hillsborough River, Prince Edward Island, putting in half a kilometre too far upstream. The Island's north-south drainage divide is close to the North Shore), where the water was very shallow and overhung with thick living brush. We next paddled in tidal waters past Mount Stewart and on down to the City of Charlottetown; this was after we participated in a colourful joint Mi'kmaq/Islander celebration of the River's long heritage and membership in the CHRS.

We then spent two days paddling down the Margaree River in Cape Breton, from high up its Northeast Branch on the edge of the Cape Breton Highlands. We descended this gorgeous Appalachian River, with its many light gravel rapids, passed sport salmon fishermen practising "catch and throw back," complete with waders, down to tidewater, then under the bridge and out onto the Northumberland Strait.

Memorable experiences on these rivers are captured in selections from Carol's log on the trip as follows:

July 6, Day 3: On the Shelburne, NS:

...Lunch on a south shore point of Irving Lake. Then it was onto the river again. It took all afternoon till about 7:30 p.m. to reach the bridge campsite where the Shelburne flows into Sand Lake.

This was the hardest part of our overall three rivers' trip, but quite tolerable. Beautiful streams, wonderful vistas, quite a bit of in and out of the canoes, a little hauling and lifting, no portaging. Lots of fun. Lots of twists and turns. Indian Falls is about three-quarters of the way down. The marked road on the map is now but a trace, no bridge, and the chute not really a falls, just a shallow class III rapids, without much power. We lowered our way down most of Indian Falls, in our boats. The Scotts had a bit of trouble, as Mary was standing in the water, tired and having some trouble manoeuvring. But she was smiling and all right. Still, Bruce thought at 6:00 p.m., with the group tired, that all should stop on river right, up the old roadway to a clearing—clearly a B-site. Most did not like this and urged us to try to reach the next bridge, about 3 km away. So we did, and it was not hard. The site on river right, by the roadway (no traffic) was gorgeous and roomy. Clearly A+.

Though tired, the morale was extra good. Huge dinner prepared by Meaghan and Carol—chickpea curry, salad and three-step tomato soup. Lots of fun. Bed about 10:30.

July 11, Day 1: On the Hillsborough, PEI

...We put in half a kilometre too far upstream by a bridge at Cherry Hill. The River was about two metres wide and it was very shallow. It had not been cleared so the first 500 metres were difficult—a lot of lifting, pulling, removing deadfall and beaver

The group paddling on the Shelburne River in Nova Scotia.

cuts, and it rained most of the day. Slowly the route improved, the river widened to perhaps 8 metres, and the bush gave way to marsh, grasses and swamp.

Then we entered a much larger, long bay-like stretch, clearly at tide-head. Beautiful shore lines, many birds, some headwinds.

July 12: "Hillsborough River Heritage Day"
...met other canoeists and Committee Members including John Hughes, of course, plus Fred Horne (Chair), Muriel Fitzpatrick, David Mills (an ex-student of Bruce's) and the female Parks Canada representative.

John Hughes had his wood-canvas voyageur canoe—9 person, perhaps 23 foot. Some of our people paddled in the voyageur canoe. There were about five other canoes in our flotilla. We paddled about five km to "the monument" on the river right, up on the shore, across the Confederation Heritage Trail to the heritage site beside the highway, with a panoramic view of the river and its shore. The River is now about one km wide and of course, is tidal.

Mi'kmaq women were delivering messages and leading the ceremonies when we arrived at the CHRS plaque….On the way down the River we saw eagles, and lots of herons especially numerous (hundreds) in a rookery on a big island along the riverside. They made quite a fuss as we stopped to look and as we paddled by….

July 14, Day 1: On the Margaree River, Cape Breton, NS

Up at about 7:30, breakfast in the Pearsons' room. Then, with Del Muise (a Cape Breton historian friend of Bruce's who met us) offering help as a shuttle driver of his car, we drove upstream, past the Forks and up by the Northeast Branch to Portree, a very tiny community at a crossing as far up as Del and others thought would be navigable… Glorious weather, clear or with light clouds, warm, bright sun. Here was exquisite highland scenery, with huge forested stretches on each side of this deep valley. We spent the day paddling the Northeast Margaree. We had barely enough water to get through the shallow stretches between the deep salmon pools. There were several shallow class II rapids….We passed a dozen or more solitary fishers, standing and fly fishing in the pools, none talkative, most briefly pleasant, only one having caught a fish. We saw numerous bald eagles, terns, kingfishers, redwing blackbirds, and a couple of osprey.

Somewhat below the fish hatchery, the River and valley widened out; there were fewer large rocks to avoid. There were still gravel bars, and the river did some braiding so one had to look for the deepest channel.

July 15 Day 2:

...The River continued in the fashion we had experienced the previous afternoon until just before Margaree Forks—the exact location of which is hard to determine due to the heavy braiding and the tall marsh grasses. We passed perhaps a dozen more fishers, even less talkative than those of the previous day. We paddled on to the bridge by Margaree Centre... and entered our long final paddle to the sea. The River was now quite wide in places, more than a km. and with several islands. The banks of the valley were still high and beautiful, but the valley was now more populated with homes and coastal roads...more eagles and more shore birds. We paddled against a light headwind, and soon the tide was in our favour, we paddled under the Cabot Trail hwy. at Margaree Harbour and out toward Belle Cote sand spit. We continued between the buoyed breakwater at the mouth of the harbour and out onto the Gulf of St. Lawrence where we rode the gentle rollers onto the beach.

Elizabeth Beaton, whom Bruce had met at Canadian Studies meetings in Ottawa a few weeks earlier, suggested we go to a Ceilidh (a performance of Gaelic folk music) after we had dinner. It was being held at the Nornaway Barn. It was a lovely way to spend our last evening, hearing some great Gaelic music. The musicians were well-known Cape Bretoners, and one of them was Jerry Holland (a fiddler strongly rooted in Cape Breton, Scottish and Irish music traditions. His music remains very influential wherever Celtic music is played. He was launching a new CD. Other players included Scott Macmillan, Allan Dewar and David MacIsaac, and a singer Bryan, from Halifax did a nice rendition "Off Cape St. Mary's."

What a contrast between our two paddling experiences in 1988! The first was far to the southwest in kayaks along the beautiful coast of the Sea of Cortez and the second on three very different rivers of the Maritime provinces.

# 34

## MORE BAJA SEA KAYAKING AND
## BACK TO THE LADY EVELYN, 1999

This was our third winter kayak trip on the Sea of Cortez. The route was similar to our first one taken in 1997. From Loreto, we paddled north along the coast, crossed over to Isla Coronadas and then made the rather long crossing south to the large Isla el Carmen. We followed its coastline southwest for its full length, then crossed over and paddled along the east side of the adjacent Isla Danzante. From there we paddled back to the mainland at Puerto Escondido. Jim Demlar was the senior leader and wrote the log. Shawn Hodgins and Liz McCarney met us in Loreto, having just led a trip just before ours. As we sat in the Café Olé with our group the day before the trip began we realized it was a Gabriola tradition. What a great idea to sit and relax and get a feeling for all those we would be with, twenty-four hours a day, for the next six days. Others on the trip were Phil and Cathy Huggins, along with their close friends, Fred and Sue Najork from Newburgh, New York. Fred and Phil had been with us on the 1997 Thelon trip. New to trip with us were friends Elissa Gershon and Kristin Lamson from San Francisco and Michael Enns from British Columbia.

We began our first day paddling out into a dense bank of fog. However, it soon lifted and we were thrilled to see the beautiful view before us. We were very much looking forward to the adventure ahead.

Excerpts from Jim's log follow:

March, Day 6: "To and on Isla Danzante"
We rose with the dawn, and Phil Huggins raced up onto the plateau (of southern Isla el Carmen) to catch another spectacular sunrise. A number of us paid homage to the rising sun, testimony to the fact that we were up with the sun, which is not hard to find when you go to bed when it sets. A rich breakfast of egg and chorizo tacos, our gratitude to Cathy and Phil Huggins, some extra coffee, and we were once again in our boats, this time on a crossing to Isla Danzante.

The crossing was uneventful and calm, but the shore of Danzante was something else. We spent a couple of hours along its shoreline in and out of rocks, gazing at the abundant life below. Time once again stood still as we lost track of it.

We lunched on artichoke pasta and other delectables, muchas gracias to Elissa Genshon and Kristin Lamson. Then we imbibed a most decadent "afternoon Margarita," swam, snorkelled and explored. Out to sea again we travelled the east side of the island, then made our way further south rounding the point and heading back north, up the west side of Danzante, past large cormorants basking in the sun. We later camped on the north west side of Danzante. Small lizards joined us for margaritas beneath the shade of our tarp.

Then another fine meal, compliments of Carol and Bruce. It seemed that whenever you turned around Carol was offering some kind of dried delicacy. Makes you feel welcome doesn't it! Anyway, the evening went like this. We told each other daring half truths about ourselves and others, played a final game of Sosolito 10,000, and called it a night, falling asleep beneath a sky of stars. This was our last night.

It was another amazing trip. We enjoyed the warm and sunny weather with the blue skies. We were thrilled to see ten to fifteen whales and some sea lions one morning. To beat the winds we always got up early, and sometimes had to take a break or stop early if too windy, but then some would read while others hiked. On one hike up into the high hills and across the Isla el Carmen, we were surprised when we came to a cliff to suddenly look out and in the distance see a huge coastal salt operation.

At other times we swam or did a small amount of snorkelling or just walked along a beach exploring. Like children we would overturn stones and pick up shells and peek into caves. We saw turkey vultures devouring a dolphin, the bones of a whale washed up on the shore and a large osprey's nest.

When the trip was over Bruce and I stayed for another week and bicycled around the town and nearby area. We met up with some Alberta fishers where we were staying. They had just caught some very nice large fish and invited us to a barbecue that evening. The next day, together, we rented a van, drove up into the hills and across the peninsula on very narrow twisty roads. Part way there we stopped to visit in a very tiny village, a Jesuit Mission. People were in the process of restoring the gold gilt throughout the interior of a large church. They had already been working on it for a couple of years and still had several years to go. On the west side of the peninsula we went out in a tour boat on the Pacific Ocean for more whale-watching. In all, a wonderful and relaxing two-week experience and we would love to return to Baja again.

In late August, we (Carol and Bruce) took a  trip to the Lady Evelyn and Maple Mountain, using the short circle route. We paddled with David McNab and Ute Lischke, to the Mountain, climbing it and returning. Great fun and glorious weather.

What a splendid way to end the paddling trips for 1999!

# PART FIVE:

# THE NEW MILLENNIUM AND
# NEW ADVENTURES, 2000–2007

# 35

## THE HAIDA GWAII, BRITISH COLUMBIA, AND THE LADY EVELYN, 2000

In July 2000, we arrived in Sandspit on Haida Gwaii by plane, then had the pleasure of travelling mainly on the motor schooner *Anvil Cove*, owned by Keith and Barbara Rowsell. Keith had been a long time Wanapitei camper who, in 1961, was on the first James Bay trip, the one led by John Scott and Bruce. Our excellent cook was Sherry Burton, a highly informed Haida who in the autumn would be returning to university. Altogether we were eleven persons, including crew. We visited most of the deserted Haida villages monitored by Haida Watchmen. Using the schooner as a base, we kayaked through narrow channels and to many beach landings. At night we, along with Ilona Bell, Karen Herold, Lynn and Jody Stockfish, camped on a beach while the others slept on the boat.

Archaeological evidence indicates man has lived here for at least 6,000 years. The first site we visited  going south at Louise Island or nearby was the Shedans village (ex-Koona) site.  Friendly Haida Watchwomen conducted our tour of fallen-in-homes and longhouses, totems, memorial and mortuary poles, the latter with their boxes for the bones up high (for chiefs only). Ninety percent of the Haida died in the smallpox epidemics of the 1880s, some earlier in the 1840s and 1860s.  We did less kayaking than expected because there was so much to see and with so much interesting history. While there, we took advantage of the opportunity available.

Moving south, we motored along the coast of Lyell Island, near the area where the clashes took place in the mid-1980s involving the

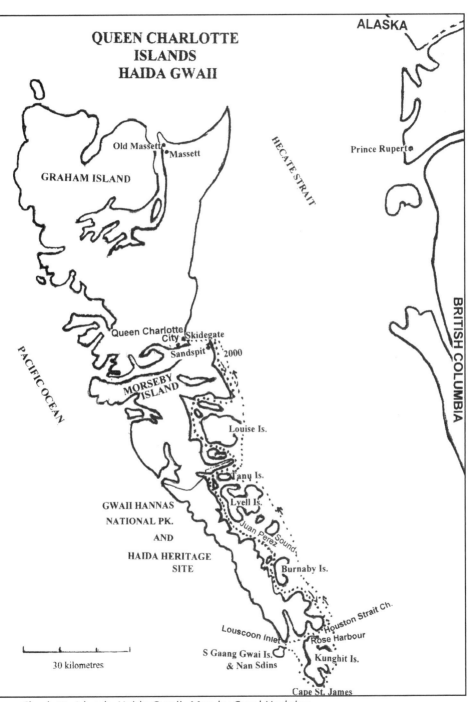

Queen Charlotte Islands: Haida Gwaii. *Map by Carol Hodgins.*

loggers, the Haida and the environmentalists. Fortunately, this led to the establishment of the National Park and negotiations toward a final Agreement Treaty with the Haida. We continued to the southern tip of Morseby Island and around Cape St. James and up the west coast as far as Louscoon Inlet. The island formerly known as Anthony Island is a World Heritage Site (1981), containing the abandoned village area of Ninstints, the richest of the Haida ruins, where once twenty longhouses stood. The two Haida women who guided us were excellent.

Next we cut through the Inlet past Rose Harbour to the east side of Morseby and headed back north. Carol's log provides a glimpse of one idyllic day:

> July 8, Day 4:
> At 8:00 a.m. Keith, in the Zodiac, picked up the six of us, (Karen Herold, Ilona Bell, Lynn and Jody Stockfish, Carol and Bruce), camped on the beach in Louscoon Inlet. Soon thereafter, from the *Anvil Cove*, we saw a black bear walk through that campsite and along the shore right where our tents had been. We went in close to shore in our kayaks to take pictures of the bear who was only interested in digging and eating the shellfish.
>
> We kayaked until

The remains of very old totem poles among the ruins of abandoned Haida villages decimated by the smallpox epidemics of the 1840s, 1860s and 1880s.

1:30 p.m., crossing Louscoon Inlet from west to east, passed Cape Fanny, paddling northeast away from the open Pacific through most of Houston Stewart Strait (between Morseby and Kunghit). *Anvil Cove*, after securing more fresh water north of Louscoon, finally caught up with us for a very late lunch. The kayaks were hoisted aboard. Then we all motored past Rose Harbour and north again all the way to Ramsay Island and the Hot Springs at Gandle K'in. Ute Lischhke, Jenifer Babe, Lyn and Jody stayed on board with the crew while Karen, Ilona, Carol and Bruce set up camp on Ramsay Island before we all had dinner on the *AC*. All except Barbara went over to Gandle K'in by Zodiac with Keith and Sherry.

There were two small black-tailed deer eating leaves of the salal bushes right beside one of the hot tubs. We had a hot soap rinse in a small shack with a hot tub with proper drains in it. We then went into three outdoor hot pools (each with stone circular walls). The tubs were different temperatures, and one had to walk on open trails over rock and through some flowers and bushes between the pools. The third pool was very close to the shore and had an ocean view out over Hecate Strait. Great fun. Carol, Jody and Ute had a quick dip in the ocean. The trail between where the Zodiac had beached and the Hot Springs was several hundred metres long, among some very large trees. The watchman and his family were living on site. Bed about 10:30 p.m.

We also visited Hik'yah at Windy Bay. This was a long fruitful visit to see the remains of several longhouses. This was the organizational site for the 1984–85 protests, and the centre for the Haida Board of Watchmen (Watchwomen). There, the trees were huge, red cedar and sika spruce. One red cedar they claimed to be 900 years old. It took nine of us with outstretched arms to circle the tree. It was awesome.

At this site a Haida elder threw hunks of halibut into the air and two eagles would come swooping down and catch them.

The last site we visited was Tanu Village where we had our most extensive tour of the remains. It had been the largest village with twenty-four longhouses. No poles remained standing. Here we saw the gravesite of Bill Reid who died in 1998. He was the greatest of the sculptors of the recent Haida cultural revival. Both cedar totem poles and huge dugout cedar canoes are again being built in Skidegate where we saw the creative Haida at work.

Paddling in Hecate Strait we could examine so much rich sea life and were fortunate to observe ten to fifteen humpback whales and a very large colony of seals, some sitting on the rocks while others frolicked in the sea. On a rocky island we saw, possibly hundreds, of sea lions, many young. Other interesting sightings were puffins and eagles—so much to see and far too little time.

Later that year, in September, following a fly-in from Wanapitei with John Milloy, Molly Blyth and John and Mary Scott, we paddled down the Lady Evelyn River from Macpherson Lake. After Divide (or Katherine Lake) our route again took us down the South Channel to Willow Island Lake and the Dew Drop campsite on Lady Evelyn Lake. From there we paddled back to Wanapitei via Diamond Lake.

> September 2, Day 3:
> Up about 7:30 a.m. at Bridal Veil Falls; we walked and then paddled back to Hap Wilson's cabin at Twin Falls[2] where we had been invited for breakfast. We were served a huge and leisurely breakfast. We had lots of interesting conversation.
>
> We left about 10:50, returning to Bridal Veil Falls,

carried the canoes, then packed up and portaged the gear. The total carry is 450 metres. The final steep descent of canoes and gear and some of the people was done collectively, with the help of the throw rope attached to a big tree. Away about 1:00 p.m., paddling down to the 900 metre "good portage" on river left around the long rapids complex, often run with lift-overs in empty canoes during spring and July high water. Several of us took three trips over the carry. We had a huge late picnic lunch at the end, about 3:00 p.m.

Paddled on to "Fat Man's Squeeze," landed easily on the left, avoiding being too close to the brink of the Falls. All but the descent of the 115-metre carry is relatively easy and open. But the "Squeeze" is steep, over broken rocks, and it is hard. Again we used the affixed throw rope. Paddling on downstream, we passed one difficult, shallow rapids and let down. Mary walked for 150 metres. Some pushed through; some had to get out. We were soon racing dusk. We didn't like the old Barn site (junky and now with no building, of course). We passed the "three miler" and landed on the left side of Willow Island Lake at a beautiful, granite, and treed site. We rushed to set up tents and light the fire. Cooked dinner in the dark. Tired, but what a day! High morale.

September 3, Day 4:
…Light rain, which continued and became slightly heavier, and visibility was not good. The females put on their rain gear. John M, and Bruce, although urged to do so did not feel it necessary. Paddled north on Willow Island to the area of the portage into "Puddle Lake," but unfortunately missed the small bay. Reversed and found a new landing for the portage slightly south of the old and somewhat

clogged area. By this time John was really shivering and getting close to having hypothermia with Bruce not far behind. We landed quickly and got a fire going and a tent up so the "cold ones" could change and get warm.

John S, Mary and Molly all working hard; Carol made some hot soup, to go with the sandwiches for lunch and then everyone had a rest. After lunch we carried canoes and gear over the portage and paddled the puddle. Portaged through the muck of the first half, then the smooth middle and the final metres of the jagged creek bed boulders. Paddled off into south end Lady Evelyn Lake looking for a campsite. The first (and best) was on the classic, small Dew Drop Island with the hard shield landing and the steep ascent to the site—the Scotts landed and set up on the far back side. Tents were set up in the dusk (about 8:00 p.m.) and dinner cooked in the dark, amid rather high north winds blowing south between the islands from far up the Lake. All in bed about 10:00, tired but happy.

Our route was similar to what we had paddled and portaged as a small part of our first three trips together as paddling partners, away back in 1957, 1958 and 1959. Happily, the Lady Evelyn River looked the same in 2000 as it had in 1957—though upstream from Macpherson Lake there had recently been a small fire along the banks. We were young adults then, well over forty years ago. Since 2000, we have not been back, and sadly, probably will not be back. Its beauty and its memories haunt us still.

# 36

## OBABIKA SHORT CIRCLE ROUTE: BACK TO THE KUUJUAQ (SOPER) RIVER, BAFFIN ISLAND, NUNAVUT, 2001

In mid-summer Bruce went on a four-day Temagami area trip out of Wanapitei, with Sandra Gillis, a close friend of ours, a former student of Bruce's and long connected with Wanapitei, Wayne Potts, a Teme Augama Anishnabai, a school principal and former Wanapitei staff and also a friend, and Ian Huggett. They canoed around the Diamond-Wakimika-Obabika-Shishkong Loop, most of which we had frequently paddled on different trips over the past forty-five years. In this little nostalgia voyage the weather was extremely hot, and they paddled under clear blue skies.

In August, we were headed out for our third Arctic trip on the Soper, this time sharing the leadership with Sharon and Larry Pearson. The group also included the Maughans (Rosemary and Robin), the Van Loons (Claire and David), and the Sines (Liz and Ian). The Park authorities of Katannilik Territorial Park (now in Nunavut) had assigned us Billy Akavak, a sophisticated Inuit, as an "armed guide"—because a disturbingly aggressive polar bear had recently been at the Soper Falls Campsite and injured two of four campers from Quebec. This was very unusual, but we were pleased to have Billy's company and he added so much to our enjoyment of the trip.

The following excerpt is taken from Carol's log "Fleming Hill and Valley":

> August 18, Day 8:
> Our first night without rain, we awoke to sunshine. Liz and Ian served us pancakes. At 9:30 we paddled a few hundred metres up the small stream and started our hike. Within minutes we came to the same meandering stream. Some folks went back, paddled the canoes to pick the rest up to be ferried across, and the hike continued over a section of flat tundra. We then began our climb to the top of Fleming Hill.[3] We zigzagged our way up from one small alpine meadow (very small covering over the limestone rock). There were lots of boulders and loose rock. It was very windy but there were many sheltered areas where we could relax. There were lots of tundra plants, small flowers, berries and caribou skeletons to examine. Near the top a caribou was spotted. At 10:45 a.m. all of us reached the summit, a small windy plateau with an Inuksuk on top, which we had seen from many km. upstream and which we again saw the next day as we paddled downstream. Some of us contributed small rocks to the Inuksuk. Although Billy had, in winter, driven through the cut behind Fleming Hill by snowmobile, this was his first climb to the top. There was lots of picture taking with the 360° panoramic view.
>
> Usually our last campsite is the one at Soper Falls, but because of the polar bear attack on the Quebec canoeists/campers about two weeks before, we were planning to spend a second night at the same site. From our terrific view, high up on Fleming, I had spied a delightful looking waterfalls further up the small stream. Since it was still too early for lunch I suggested we go back to our canoes and paddle to these falls.

Billy Akavak, shooting rapids. Billy was a very personable Inuit who accompanied us.

Sharon and I hiked along the bank and were then ferried across just below. We lunched in a small, relatively flat sheltered rock nook overlooking the falls beside where the stream flowed through a small limestone gorge. It was delightful. Naturally, Sharon and Larry investigated further upstream, to the top of the next hill, but had left their camera behind at the lunch spot. Following lunch, Liz and Ian walked back to a spot opposite our campsite and were picked up by one of our canoes to be taken "home." While waiting for their pick-up, a caribou walked nearby, swam across the river and pranced through our campsite. The Pearsons and Maughans with me tagging along, hiked back up the hill behind and then up another hill. By now we were just north, on the opposite side of the Soper River, from the grey limestone hills of the mica and lapis lazuli. From here we could see far up the Soper River Valley as well as another valley upriver of our lunch spot. "Awesome views." Sharon and Larry paddled both remaining canoes back to our campsite while Robin, Rosemary and I went overland on a variation of the route taken by Liz and Ian. We did a lot of bog jumping. Within minutes of our arrival on the shore opposite our campsite, Ian was there in his "taxi" canoe.

Meanwhile Billy and Dave had paddled 2.5 km. down the Soper to see who was camped there. From the top of Fleming we had seen a motorboat and some people. Billy was sure he would know them and he thought that he and Dave could get a ride back in the outboard. He indeed did know them. One of the women was his aunt, and there were several children. Dave enjoyed his first slice of raw Arctic Char. The "eyes," loved by the children, are considered a delicacy. The Inuit men were down fishing by Soper Falls so Dave and Billy had the hard paddle back upstream against the current, but the two of them thoroughly enjoyed their surprise visit.

While most were away from the campsite, Bruce, who returned following the hike to Fleming Hill, had a sleep, Later, Liz cleaned up and served Bruce tea in his tent, and Ian cleaned our Coleman stove. The Van Loons were on dinner. Claire said she had a quick, simple dinner. It was delicious, scalloped potatoes and a pasta dish. All hands helped to clean up our equipment. During the trip Dave had his hands in the dishpan following most meals. An inventory was done of equipment to be left in Iqaluit. I had cinnamon buns for the last morning's menu, not a great idea with clean-up and inventory, [too time consuming] and the fact that it began to rain lightly. I mixed them up but decided to just make a bannock in two layers with the cinnamon in between. Billy did the baking for me. The rain did stop. All were in bed by 9:00 p.m.

Baffin Island is a common destination but not for canoeists. It is better known for its hiking further north at Pangnirtung. Most who have canoed the Soper River love it, but there are not many organized trips available. However, it is one of the closest places from Ottawa or Montreal where one can truly be in the Arctic. Following are some of Liz Sine's reflections from her first wilderness trip to the Arctic, this one with us:

Day 1-Aug. 11: Mount Joy
I have to pinch myself to see if I am dreaming. It's 9:40 p.m. and I'm sitting on the steep hillside just above our row of 6 colourful domed tents.  As I raise my eyes across the flat terrace to the Soper River, I see our kitchen area—4 barrels, 2 wanajins [wanagans], Coleman stove protected from wind by the upturned canoe, green kitchen tarp.

I look up the steep rise to the ridge across the river–tomorrow's hiking goal.  To my left is the esker on which our twin Otter made a very scary landing— pilot and co-pilot both displayed some dismay as we ploughed deep ruts in the gravel safely in time... After dinner a 2-hour hike over rough tundra (boots an absolute necessity) up to Panorama Falls—spectacular. A truly spiritual experience, sitting perched on a rock just letting the feelings and awesome vista sink in.  Raven winging their way along the cliff tops loudly protest our presence.  Saw 8 caribou in ones, twos and threes, trotting over the tundra with their amazing floating gait. Many antlers, caribou bones and droppings are scattered on the hillsides.  We came upon a tent ring of moss and low bush covered stones. Billy tells us it's from an Inuit hunt camp of hundreds of years ago.

It's very different to be above the tree line; looking far up river valleys and listening to tumbling water in the Soper River.  Never have we been in such a wilderness setting. Being with experienced outdoor people, it feels good just to be here...

# 37
## DAY-TRIP PADDLING, 2002

With the new year, we continued paddling with our Peterborough-based spring Canoe Group on a combination of simple and complex local rivers. These included the lower Indian, the lower Salmon, the lower Moira, the Irondale, the Opeongo (out of Algonquin Park), Eel's Creek, and sometimes the Mississauga, the Snake Rapids section of the Madawaska and more recently, the Minesing Swamp of the lower Nottawasaga River.

Bruce wrote a descriptive account about all these trips in his "No-Name Trent-Peterborough Canoe Group: A Whimsical History—1966 to 2001," which became part of Alistair Thomas's book, *More of Canada's Best Canoe Routes*.[4]

We also continued in 2002 with summer and autumn day trips out of Wanapitei, Temagami. We thought that perhaps we had retired from the longer, northern canoe voyages, but our paddling partnership certainly was not about to end.

# 38
## THE BLOODVEIN RIVER IN
## NORTHERN MANITOBA, 2003

On this trip in July 2003, we were only "honorary leaders." Besides the two of us, the group included our great friends, all now veteran trippers with us: Lynda and Don Mason, Cathryn Rees and Bill Cormode, (these four had planned and packed the trip), and Leila and Jack Nessen. We flew in, eastward from Biscuit Lodge, four kilometres south of Pine Dock, on the west coast of Lake Winnipeg, north of Gimli. Our plane landed on the Bloodvein River, near the Manitoba's border with Ontario.

The Bloodvein is a beautiful Canadian Heritage River found in both provinces (It rises near Red Lake, Ontario). It flows west through typical Shield country almost to its mouth at the narrows on Lake Winnipeg. At the end of the trip from the Cree village, also called Bloodvein, we took the free ferry the twenty-two kilometres across the lake back to its west side.

We had left our cars at Biscuit Lodge, which was about fifteen kilometres south of there, and where we had stayed the night before the trip. From the Lodge we flew in a Northway Aviation float plane to our put-in on the Bloodvein River. (The aviation company also owned the lodge.) The River has many light and heavy rapids, and a few falls, but no long portages. Still, it is "remote." We were on it for only a week.

Along with the usual topographical maps, we used *Wilderness Rivers of Manitoba*[5] by Hap Wilson and Stephanie Ackroyd. The numbering of the falls, as found in the excerpt from Carol's log that follows, came from their account.

July 18, Day 5: To Namay Falls

The morning was hot, and the afternoon hotter. We left the campsite at 7:20 a.m. We had another scenic day ahead, beginning with a twisting three-quarter kilometre paddle; first rapids, #74, we did a lift-over, the portage ending in a narrow rock area. We saw another eagle, which might have been a golden. Next came several swifts and a rapid, Little Birch Falls, a canyon rapids, all a beautiful sight from the high cliff overlooking the river. We portaged on the right. We saw a very, very old twisted, knotted Jack pine at the end of a portage. The top had been knocked off; the tree was probably 200 years old. We then shot an easy R I and paddled over the remains of an old winter-road bridge. Cribs could be seen under the water. After another obstacle, Ankuazi Falls was bypassed by a short portage. We were looking forward to a nice easy lift-over. Wrong! There was lots of water running through a narrow drop. At the end of the easy portage we had to lower the canoes down a rock face.

Lunch on the banks of the Bloodvein River.

We met up again with the Camp Pinecrest canoe trip just after the portaging. They ran the rapids, #80 Namay Falls, Pinecrest taking the short portage on the left. We took the much longer portage to a campsite with lots of tent spots in a big open area among the Jack pine. We did have to scramble down a rocky path for water. Near the end of the portage we had a nice swimming area, enjoyed by all. It was very hot with a light breeze. Great evening—beef Bourgogne for dinner. Eagles, golden eye ducks, and night hawks were among our bird sightings.

As noted before, the Bloodvein is a beautiful river. It is also, however, a particularly important river for seeing and studying ancient pictographs. We liked it and so did a Wanapitei youth group, which in 2005 ran the entire route beginning just west of Red Lake, Ontario. The Bloodvein was an excellent choice to be named to the Canadian Heritage Rivers System. We thoroughly enjoyed the voyage, but Bruce was tiring on the portages, often getting help from Bill Cormode and often needing a sleep before dinner. There was trouble ahead.

# 39

## AGAIN ONLY DAY-TRIP PADDLING, 2004–2005

B ruce suffered a relatively severe heart attack in February 2004. Following seven weeks in hospital and the insertion of four stents (the procedure accomplished at the Ottawa Heart Institute), his blood flow increased significantly. However, he has been left with an aneurysm in the wall of the left ventricle. Therefore, he was medically advised not to portage canoes or do any heavy lifting.

Our spring Canoe Group by the Salmon River (standing l-r); Bill Cormode, Barry Diceman, Nicola Jennings, Jen Deck, Dave Goslin and Larry Hodgins; (sitting l-r): Heather Dunlop, Cathryn Rees, Bruce, Carol, John Jennings and Ted Moores. *Photo by Claudette (Languedoc) Kohut.*

In May 2004, Bryan Poirier, a former Trent student of Bruce's, and a Wanapitei Camp and adult trip leader, brought Bruce back to the canoe. The first paddle, with Bruce in the bow that year was a spring outing around Little Lake in Peterborough, with a bit on the Otonabee River. Then, after attending a Canadian Heritage Rivers Conference in Guelph, the two of them paddled the Grand River with a flotilla of over twenty boats from the conference, cruising down from Cambridge to Paris, Ontario, amid lots of broad class I rapids. It felt wonderful!

That summer, at Wanapitei on Lake Temagami, we (Carol and Bruce) went on evening and day paddles on the Red Squirrel River and about Ferguson Bay. We also went up into Red Squirrel Lake and into Sharp Rock Inlet, with others doing the carrying.

In 2005 that pattern continued, and we also participated as canoeing partners in the easier spring whitewater runs of the Canoeing Group on parts of the Indian, Salmon, Moira, Irondale and lower Opeongo rivers Then came more extensive day trips out of Wanapitei. Bruce was definitely back in the swing of things. We were continuing as paddling partners.

# 40

## NORTH GEORGIAN BAY AND
## PHILIP EDWARD ISLAND, 2006

In the spring of 2006 we participated with our Canoeing Group in the usual whitewater day trips. During July we went on a one-week canoe trip with John and Nicola Jennings, Bill Cormode and Cathryn Rees. Our put-in was on the small Chikanishing Creek east of Killarney village, on the rugged northern coast of Georgian Bay. From there we paddled across the western end of Collins Inlet and out around the jagged edges of Philip Edward Island, heading further east. We camped on various small rocky islands and took in several exploratory hikes on the islands, one into the interior of Philip Edward itself.For most of the trip the weather was fantastic, blue skies, warm temperatures and with light breezes. On July 17 we went for an afternoon hike to the top of the small island on which we were camped; we had a panoramic view of that part of the northern Georgian Bay area. However, there was a haze, and Cathryn felt something was very strange about it.

On our return, part way down the hill toward our gorgeous but exposed campsite, we saw a narrow black band across the whole southern sky. Thinking that a rainstorm was approaching, we hurried back to the campsite, about ten minutes away, and began putting up some kitchen tarps. Before the first tarp was fully secured we were hit by a terrific storm, "a micro-burst," causing the uprooting of large, very old white pines that had grown on very shallow soil on top of the granite. The island was typical, semi-barren granite rock of the Shield. Cathryn in the nick of time, collapsed Bill's and her tent. Bill, who happened to be nearby, saw our two canoes, which had been tied together in a sheltered area, being picked up and blown out into the Bay. They were tossed around as if they were in an eddy. He quickly waded into the water up to his hips and was able to grab one of the rope painters and pull the canoes back in. All this time it was raining and blowing, with heavy thunder and lightening. Pretty scary.

Our tent was blown into the bushes, although it had gear and many small rocks inside, and rocks on all the guy lines outside. We ran and jumped on it, and with our bodies and outstretched arms tried to keep it down. Cathryn's and Bill's golden retriever Sofie was terrified, so we put her between us, as parts of the tent were wildly flapping. The tent fly was ripped, and the tent itself was covered with tiny pin holes.

During this time John and Nicola's canoe was blown about thirty feet away, fortunately only into the bushes. They were in their tent, and it collapsed on them. They had to lie on their backs with their feet up, holding onto the poles to try and keep the tent from also being blown away. To make matters worse, water was running

Bill Cormode and Cathryn Rees (foreground) and Bruce and Carol paddling on Chikanishing, a creek that flows between the Killarney Road and Collins Inlet, Georgian Bay. *Photo by John Jennings.*

into their tent. In about fifteen terrifying minutes, which seemed much more, the storm was over, but it took some time for the waves to abate. We actually ended the day with a lovely evening with a beautiful sunset.

The next day we moved northwest amongst the islands to our last campsite following a narrow corridor of fallen trees. The following noon after our paddle back to our cars, we drove into the village of Killarney where the docks and many of the yachts tied to them had suffered considerable damage from the fast-rising water levels. We were told that there had been approximately two-thirds of a metre surge of water pouring through Killarney Channel.

Along with Nicola and John, we bought lunch at the famous Harbours Fish and Chips stand. We then, Bruce and Carol, visited with Daryl, Warren and Isolde Hodgins, staying the night at their cottage on Goat Island in Killarney Bay, where over the years so many Wanapitei groups coming from the Camp have ended their voyages, all stretching back to that first canoe trip from Temagami to Killarney in 1960.

# 41

## SEA KAYAKING ON THE BAY OF EXPLOITS, NEWFOUNDLAND; BACK ON GEORGIAN BAY, 2007

In mid-July, we went on a six-day kayaking trip on the Bay of Exploits on the north-central coast of Newfoundland. This trip was organized by Wanapitei C.A.N.O.E., and (our guide and son) Shawn Hodgins met our group at the Gander airport. After shopping for last minute items, we travelled to Lawrence Harbour, locally known as "Lawrence Hole," where our Newfoundland contact, the other guide and co-leader, Paul Langdon bases his company, Canoe Hill Adventures, Sea Kayaking on the Bay of Exploits.

Paul is a certified kayak instructor and along with his assistant Jason Folkes, and Shawn, we had three great leaders. Our fellow participants were Molly Blyth, Marilyn Job, Meredith and Elliot Rodger, Cathy Robinson, Jim Sculthorpe and Rod Williamson.

Following a good night's sleep we travelled in Paul's fishing boat, the *Adonis*, to the Exploits Islands. Paul provided maritime navigation instruction throughout the crossing. Once we reached the Exploits, we pitched our tents near a cabin owned by Paul. This was to be our base where we would do our cooking.

The remainder of the day was spent honing our sea kayaking skills. Although a few of the participants had some kayaking experience, they were thrilled to be with such experienced, conscientious, capable and dedicated leaders. Some passed their basic level of certification.

We were quite familiar with Shawn's capable paddling skills, but were delighted to find Paul and Jason expert instructors as well.

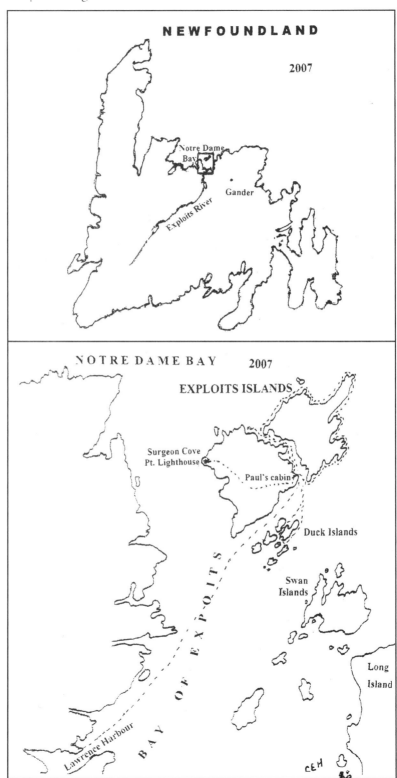

Exploits Bay, Newfoundland. *Maps by Carol Hodgins.*

True Newfoundlanders, both were most hospitable, very friendly and had a great sense of humour.

During the trip we paddled to the outer islands of the Bay of Exploits (off Notre Dame Bay) where we did day kayaking trips in and around Exploits, Burnt Exploits, Duck and Swan islands. We lunched on small beaches and did some hiking. We visited old graveyards, one now nestled in a tranquil woodland. We entered a cave among the rocky cliffs where some Beothuk skeletons had been found a number of years ago. We were screeched at by osprey gliding above their very large nests on top of craggy cliffs and by black guillemots resting on cliff ledges.

On the day that we paddled eastwards and circumnavigated Burnt Exploits Island we had high barren cliffs to our right without many places to land. To our left was the open sea stretching north towards Greenland and beyond. We paddled by a marvellous, large, beautifully sculptured iceberg. We were told that it had been there for sometime, probably caught on the ocean floor. It was a thrill to view it from a kayak.

One day we hiked six kilometres to an abandoned, now automated lighthouse high up on top of a cliff on the northwest corner of the most westerly of the Exploit Islands (the same island where the cabin and our tents were located). The weather was warm and the sea was calm, and the group had nothing but a wonderful time. The last day three of us went back to the base camp by boat with Paul while the others kayaked. The morning was sunny and there was no

Paul Langdon (top), Carol and Shawn Hodgins on the Bay of Exploits, Newfoundland. *Photo by John Folkes.*

wind, but it soon began to rain, and then become foggy. We all returned safely and happily to Lawrence Hole. That evening back at Paul's base camp, Paul's wife Joann served us a typical Newfoundland turkey dinner with salt pork and all the trimmings along with blueberry and partridge berry pies and Newfoundland blueberry and elderberry wine.

Shawn knew everyone before the trip began but no one else did, but every person did know at least two other people. Although the personalities were very different the group gelled almost immediately and every individual became interested in both the kayaking and the hiking. Meal responsibilities were shared, but there was always someone else jumping in to help. We also were very lucky with the weather. It was warm, the sea was calm and we only had rain on the last day. Every single person loved the experience.

In August 2007, for the second time, we paddled down Chikanishing Creek out of Killarney Provincial Park. In the late afternoon, with moderate wind and waves, we paddled right across the Western Entrance of Collins Inlet and around South Point. We soon found an overnight campsite high up on the pink granite rock among the large white pines and small cedar trees. There were plenty of potential sites for our four tents. Besides the two of us, the group included Nicola and John Jennings, Cathryn Rees and Bill Cormode with their golden retriever Sophie, a seasoned canoe tripper. Don Mason also had his dog Gus, also a retriever. This was Gus's first canoe trip. After he got used to the waves, Gus adjusted and loved the experience.

Don's wife Lynda had passed away in late June and we were delighted that Don agreed to join us. He is a fantastic person to have along. There were many memories for him, as he and Lynda had done numerous trips together in this same area and over the years had canoed with us on many far northern trips. They were also part of our spring Canoe Group. Since they built their "cottage" on the Irondale River, they had hosted at least four potluck dinners following a spring paddle on that river. Lynda was a terrific cook and always had something special prepared.

John, originally an Alberta boy, provided top of the line steaks for our first dinner while Nicola tossed up a delicious Greek salad, veggies and dessert. There was plenty of dry, dead wood so the steaks were barbecued on the grill and the veggies simmered on the camping stove. We then spent a leisure evening chatting around the fire.

Following breakfast and packing up on day two we paddled east among the shoals and small islands. Margaret E. Derry's book *Georgian Bay Jewel: The Killarney Bay Story*[6] makes it clear that Wikwemekong (including the former Point Grondine band) based on Manitoulin Island most likely has unsurrendered title to Philip Edward Island and all the offshore islands through which we were paddling, except for the few already patented.

The wind and waves were particularly noticeable as we crossed an open stretch to Le Hayes Island. We paddled halfway around the north side, and at the end Cathryn and Carol got out to look for a campsite—the first spot did not have enough tent sites. They walked from the rock areas, across a dry marsh and up onto the rocks again. Don and the Jenningses paddled almost the length of the south side of the island and found a small protected area It was perfect. The canoes had a safe place to be and there were many great camp sites and a protected eating area among the pines and cedars. We also had scenic views across some islands and the Bay and even better, sheltered places to swim.

The following morning we decided not to pack up but rather do a day trip and take a lunch. We continued eastward among the islands with the wind at our back past Desjardin Point. We then hiked to the top of a small island for a 360-degree view.

After our descent in the hot sun, three of us decided to go swimming. Nicola dove in, Cathryn entered the water from a tiny gravel area a few feet away and Carol slid down a sloping slippery rock and did a low dive with Sophie beside her, doing a dog jump at the same time. Nicola noticed that when Carol surfaced she was missing her prescription sunglasses; she had forgotten they were still on. They were gone and not to be seen. A few minutes later Don came over, walked into the water where Cathryn went in, did a duck dive, and later said he could not see a thing. However, he groped around with his hands and when his head popped up out of the water he was wearing the missing glasses. He received a big hug and grateful thanks. During the return to our campsite we had powerful headwinds and larger waves, so the going was hard work.

Cathryn made a delicious pasta dinner. We had wind all night so decided to stay put on Le Hayes Island another day. As much of the island had already been explored, Cathryn, Carol and Nicola decided to walk along the large rocks as close to the water as possible and find a nice swimming spot. After swimming and resting in the sun they continued the full circle around the island, and then had another swim. The others were reading or resting. That evening, we had a campfire on a large flat rock with a great

An August evening, relaxing around our campfire on Georgian Bay.

view. It had been a wonderful day. The wind died down somewhat during the wee hours.

Up early, and after packing and a quick breakfast of coffee, oranges and granola we set off and as we retraced our strokes the wind and height of the waves increased. It was particularly hard crossing some unprotected areas. We saw few canoeists. There were far more kayakers. With the wind and the waves, the water is frequently friendlier to kayakers.

Following a hard paddle, we stopped for a rest and lunch. Once more we started out again, but it was becoming too risky and there was nowhere to land, if necessary. The rocky cliffs around us were too rugged and too high. Fortunately, we found a more sheltered area across a small channel. Storm clouds were now coming, and by the time we got the canoes and gear out of the water and started to put up the tarp, we were hit by wind, rain and hail. Drenched, we safely hunkered down in a moss-covered hollow. When the storm passed, we sat in the sun and dried out. But more dark clouds covered a large part of the sky. Under the tarp, we endured a second rainstorm. When the sun came out we took the tarp down. However, in the far distance the sky did not look favourable. Up went the tarp again, and we waited out a third rain.

Once the water became much calmer, we set off. We had planned to camp on the same site as the first night, but the weather forecast (Don had a marine radio) was for more bad weather. Hence, when we reached the site we crossed the channel and paddled up the creek. We then packed up the car and drove into Killarney to eat at one of our favourite spots, Harbours Fish and Chips well-situated on the busy waterfront.

# Epilogue

What does it all mean, these fifty years of being paddling partners? The sceptic could perhaps assert that it means very little. To the two of us, we can counter that it means an incalculable amount. For our fellow participants, we hope, and for many who are now our very close friends, we know that it has meant a very great deal to them. For us it means staggeringly important experiences, seeing so much of northern Canada, much of which can only be seen up close from the canoe or on the portages, and it has deepened our knowledge of Canada's northern history. The two of us have rarely canoed-tripped alone. We have nearly always been with others. What amazing experiences! What bonding! What friendships!

None of our canoe trips have been forgotten. Helped by pictures, old and recent, trips all live on in vivid memory. We remember well that first canoe trip together in 1957, on the Lady Evelyn, with Allie Fretz and a group of teenagers. These young campers are now in their mid-sixties, and Allie just died in late August at about age ninety.

We cherish the memories of both conversation and silence around the campfire, after a hard day and by a great dinner. We remember the beauty of the rivers, the forests or the tundra, the hills, the mountains and the lowlands. We cherish the memories of glorious evenings, cool enough to ward off the bugs and thus prolong the fellowship.

Then there are the villages and hamlets of the Indigenous Peoples across the North—from the Temagami First Nation (Teme Augama Anishnabai) on Bear Island, where we have so many friends, to the Inuit of Kugluktuk, Kimmirut and Baker Lake and to so many Cree

Our group on Exploits Bay, From l-r: Paul Langdon, Carol , Molly Blyth, Bruce, Meredith Rodgers, Rod Williamson, Elliot Rodgers, Shawn Hodgins, Jom Skulthorpe, Marilyn Job, Cathy Robinson. *Photo by Meredith Roger.*

communities up the coast of James Bay, east of Moose Factory and Washkaganish, west past Fort Albany and Attawapiskat to Fort Severn. We have also visited Dene communities in the Mackenzie Valley and always found them interested and helpful. The same sentiments hold for the Indigenous Peoples in the Yukon, especially in Old Crow, and to the people of the Haida Gwaii (Queen Charlottes, BC). We thank them all. They have been so important to us personally and to our trips. Thus there is great melancholy amidst our joys and our memories, for the people and places that we may never see again.

Nor will we ever forget the paddlers of our spring Canoeing Group. Such friendships over the decades, river canoeing five or six times each spring, with lunches on the river banks, dinners at the end, big pot luck lunches before the season, and the late May weekend at the Cormode/Rees cottage on the Madawaska not far from the beloved Opeongo River. Some of the spring canoeists have been paddling with us for over thirty years, some have just joined us recently. Many of them overlap significantly with our deep wilderness excursions, with Wanapitei, with Trent, with the Canadian Canoe Museum and with our extended family.

In the end it all comes down to six words: experiences, friendships, the land, the rivers, the memories and, that sturdy little Canadian craft, the canoe, one of the "Seven Wonders of Canada."

# Notes

## Introduction

1. Bruce W. Hodgins, *Wanapitei on Temagami: A Story of Adventures, 1931–2005* (Peterborough, ON: Wanapitei, 2006).
2. Carol Hodgins, *Wanapitei Canoe Trippers' Cookbook: Wilderness Cooking for Fun and Nutrition* (Cobalt, ON: Highway Book Shop, 1982. Revised edition, 2000). *Wanapitei Canoe Trippers' Cookbook II: Wilderness Cooking for the Environment & You* (Cobalt, ON: Highway Book Shop, 1999).
3. Herb Pohl, (James Raffin, ed.) *The Lure of Faraway Places: Reflections on Wilderness and Solitude*, edited by James Raffan (Toronto: Natural Heritage Books/The Dundurn Group, 2007). See also Bruce W. Hodgins "Refiguring Wilderness: A Personal Odyssey," in *Journal of Canadian Studies*, 33:2 (Summer 1998): 12–26.

## Part One: The Tripping Together Begins, 1957–1969

1. James Edmund Jones, "Campcraft" in *Manuel for Tuxis Boys* (Toronto: Canadian Standard Efficiency Training, National Council, YMCA, 1918), 191.
2. From the 1930s until the early 1970s, nearly all Canadian youth camps and adult recreational voyageurs paddled in wood-canvas canoes. Most were made by the Chestnut Canoe Company in Fredericton, NB; other canvas-covered canoes were made close by in Old Town, Maine. Many of the Chestnuts were relabelled and marketed by the Peterborough Canoe Company. The two companies ultimately merged. Some

canvas-covered canoes were made in Temagami by the small Temagami Canoe Company. The Aboriginal People and the fur traders paddled until the twentieth century in birchbark canoes.

In Ontario and the State of New York in the early twentieth century most recreational canoe trippers used cedar-strip wooden canoes; in Ontario these were mainly made in Peterborough and along the Trent Valley. All of this and more is carefully explained in several books, especially in Jamie Benidickson, *Idleness, Water and the Canoe: Reflections on Paddling for Pleasure*. Toronto: University of Toronto Press, 1977. See also John Jennings (ed.), *The Canoe: A Living Tradition*. Toronto: Firefly Books, 2002. The Canadian Canoe Museum in Peterborough highlights all this historical use.

3.   Beginning after the Second World War the Grumman Aircraft Company moved into the making of light but strong aluminium canoes and small motor boats. Grumman captured a huge amount of the market. By the 1950s Grumman canoes had become the principal canoe for travel in the Far North. Eric Morse, the great modern voyageur, persuaded the Hudson's Bay Company to establish a system of U-Paddle canoe rentals. Recreational paddlers could rent these canoes at one Post and leave them at another. Often they would be flown back to the starting point in the autumn or winter by a plane that had brought supplies into the Post. We, however, found these canoes so unaesthetic and so noisy with the floating sand in the river water knocking on the bottom of the canoe. They easily stuck on rocks in shallow water. In the Far North they were cold to sit in. Nevertheless, we used them on the Nahanni, the Churchill and the Bell-Porcupine rivers because of their easy accessibility. Later, on many of our less rigorous trips we would first use fibreglass and then kevlar canoes because of their light weight. Nearly all of our northern river trips would settle, by the late seventies, on ABS (a rubber-like compound) canoes because of their durability, even though they were heavier.

4.   Father Charles Paradis was a famous colonizing priest in the late nineteenth and early twentieth centuries. His main

activities were in the Upper Gatineau Valley and then in northeastern Ontario. His most success settlements were around Verner, Warren, River Valley and Field. His main retreat was, however, at Sandy Lake on Lake Temagami, 1891 to 1924. In 1931, that place became the site for Camp Wanapitei.

5.   Bruce W. Hodgins, *Paradis of Temagami: The Story of Charles Paradis, 1848–1926, Northern Priest, Colonizer and Rebel* (Cobalt, ON: Highway Book Shop, 1976).

6.   In Alistair Thomas, *Paddle Quest: Canada's Best Canoe Routes* (Toronto: Boston Mills, 2000), 81.

7.   For more background information on the Temagami area, see Bruce W. Hodgins and Jamie Benidickson, *The Temagami Experience: Recreation, Resources, and Aboriginal Rights in the Northern Ontario Wilderness*. Toronto: University of Toronto Press, 1989.

8.   Bruce W. Hodgins, *Wanapitei on Temagami: A Story of Adventures* (Peterborough, ON: Wanapitei Publishing, 1996) 55–56.

9.   Such large groups would not be contemplated today because of the difficulty in finding large enough campsites, the extra time required for portaging and cooking meals and the overall environmental impact on an area. In the Temagami district we are now limited to twelve persons on a trip and in the Algonquin and Killarney parks, the limit is nine persons.

10.  Outward Bound was originally formed in Wales and at the time focused on coastal rescues from large rowboats. Today, it is a very large organization, especially in the U.S. involved in adult and late-teen rigorous outdoor education with a focus on self-knowledge and personal growth. There are two bases in Canada, one near Burk's Falls, Ontario. Both the Canadian and some of the American Outward Bound bases have wilderness canoe trips as a speciality.

**Part Two: The Adventuresome Seventies, 1970–1979**

1.   Chief Billy Diamond would go on to become the grand chief of the entire Quebec Cree Nation. He would lead

the struggle against the harnessing of the southern James Bay rivers and secure the great James Bay Agreement, the first modern Agreement with Aboriginal Peoples. The Cree received many financial benefits and a system of subsidizing persons continuing to engage in trapping and hunting. The Agreement also provided for a major, well-financed Cree school system. The price was to acquiesce in the multiple damming, further north, of the La Grande River.

In 1973, Bruce was responsible for bringing Billy Diamond to address a large faculty and student gathering in the Great Hall of Champlain College at Trent University. Today, Billy Diamond is again chief of Waskaganish, the current name for Rupert House.

2. Sweeper is the name given to a tree or large branch hanging out over or in the water, often creating a threat to canoes hugging the shore in swift current.

3. In the 1770s, Benjamin Frobisher and other Montreal-based fur traders, the future North West Company, were active in the area, then the Hudson's Bay Company built a post on the lake in 1799. In 1864, Fathers Laflèche and Taché established a Catholic mission there. Today, the small population is a mixture of Cree, Dene and Euro-Canadians.

4. Sigurd Olson, *The Lonely Land* (New York: Knopf, 1961). For more background on the Churchill River and on *The Lonely Land*, see Bruce W. Hodgins and Gwyneth Hoyle, *Canoeing North into the Unknown: A Record of River Travel, 1874 to 1974* (Toronto: Natural Heritage Books, 1994), 91–95. Second printing 1997.

5. Log excerpt used with the permission of Gwyneth Hoyle.

6. For more background on the Coppermine, see Hodgins and Hoyle, *Canoeing North into the Unknown*, 168–76.

7. George Douglas, *Lands Forlorn* (New York: Knickerbocker Press, 1914). For more background information, see Hodgins and Hoyle, *Canoeing North into the Unknown*, 20, 121, 156, 170 with photographs.

**Part Three: From Northern Ontario to the Far North, 1980–1989**

1.  The extended Katt family is the largest sub-division of the Ka ka ka Clan of the Teme Augama Anishnabai, several of whom have worked at Wanapitei. For more information on one branch of the family, see Madeline Katt Theriault, *From Moose to Moccasins: The Story of Ka Kita Wa Pa No Kwe* (Toronto: Natural Heritage Books, 1992). Reprinted 1995. Second edition 2006.

2.  Copies were typed out and put together as information for Wanapitei trippers travelling the system.

3.  For background information on the Thelon River, see David F. Pelly, *Thelon: A River Sanctuary* (Merrickville, ON: CRCA, 1996).

4.  George Whalley was a Queen's University professor of English who wrote *The Legend of John Hornby* (Toronto: Macmillan, 1962); Laurentian Library, 1977. For another perspective on John Hornby, see Gwyneth Hoyle, *The Northern Horizons of Guy Blanchet: Intrepid Surveyor, 1884–1966* (Toronto: Natural Heritage Books/The Dundurn Group, 2007).

5.  David Hanbury, *Sport and Travel in the Northland of Canada* (London: Arnold, 1904).

6.  The Lost Patrol is a reference to the time that F.J. Fitzgerald and three other Mounties starved to death on a trek from Fort McPherson to Dawson City in the winter of 1910–11.

7.  "The Spanish River Saga" by Richard Mansfield:

    > A venturesome group of canoeists
    > Were gathered one day in the North.
    > Their plan was to experience the Spanish,
    > A river of formidable worth.
    >
    > There were Brucie and Carol, the leaders,
    > A seasoned and muscular two,
    > Which is more than we can say for the others
    > That made up the colourful crew....

They finally reached Killarney,
A sad and bedraggled team.
But through it all, the mud and the rain,
They'd realized another dream.

For they shared an experience
That few had the privilege to know:
A freedom, a sense of belonging,
An opportunity to grow.

And what greater reception,
Than the one they received at the end
From Barb and Daryl at their cottage,
That they graciously offered to lend.

So lets give three cheers for our leaders
A committed and wonderful pair,
For Wanapitei and all it means
May it live for many a year.

8. For more background on the Magnetawan River and the Almaguin Highlands, see Astrid Taim, *Almaguin Chronicles: Memories of the Past* (Toronto: Natural Heritage Books/The Dundurn Group, 2007).

9. The FQCC Report refers to the publication of river maps with details concerning the level of the rapids, prepared by the Féderation québécoise de canot-camping, an organization of Quebec canoeists, mainly whitewater trippers.

10. The TWS (Temagami Wilderness Society) had been formed in the mid-1980s to focus opposition to clear-cut logging in the Temagami District. More importantly the TWS opposed the building of the trunk roads through the already protected areas especially the new Lady Evelyn-Smoothwater Provincial Park. The roads were to be built for the hauling of Old Growth pine. The key figures in the TWS were Hap Wilson, Brian Back, John Kilridge, Cathy Ingerson and

Bernine Lloyd. Carol and Bruce Hodgins were members. The TWS was, however, rather Toronto-centred. Most of the participants on this trip were from the honorary Advisory Committee. The problem was that some of the leaders of the TWS did not have very good relations with members of the Temagami First Nation, who opposed the road construction and the clear-cutting through their homeland. The TFN did not have a proper treaty. An agreement is very close now but not yet finally settled.

The story to early 1989 is told in Bruce W. Hodgins and Jamie Benidickson, *The Temagami Experience* (Toronto: University of Toronto Press, 1989), which, alas, stops before the great clashes 1989–90.

11. Ontario Hydro controls the dam at the mouth of the Lady Evelyn River and at the real outlet (below Cross Lake) of Lake Temagami.

12. The recipe for "gado gado," a dish of pasta shells with a delicious sauce, including vegetables, nuts, seeds etc. is from Carol Hodgins, *Wanapitei Canoe Trippers Cookbook II*, 40.

## Part Four: Near and Far: North and South, 1990–1999

1. These paragraphs of historical background are adapted from the opening section of the trip log by Bruce and Carol Hodgins, their record of the South Macmillan trip of 1991.

2. For more information on the CANOL Road, see Gwyneth Hoyle, *The Northern Horizons of Guy Blanchet: Intrepid Surveyor, 1884–1966.*

3. The A.R.C. Jones account is in Karpes and Pugh, *The South Macmillan Route* (Whitehorse, YK: Yukon Books), 1987. A.R.C. Jones gave us a copy of the fifteen-page memoir of his 1990 trip on the River, "Canoeing in the Yukon: A Gourmet Adventure on the South Macmillan."

4. "Methye" is the Cree word for burbot, a freshwater cod.

5. The Wilderness Canoeing Symposium is a large gathering of like-minded people who meet annually in Toronto in late January or early February on a Friday night and all day

Saturday. There are many short talks, usually illustrated with slides, now more commonly DVDs or videos, on northern travelling excursions or related topics. The key organizer is George Luste, a physics professor at the University of Toronto, himself a great northern canoe tripper and a prominent collector of northern books.

6. The river was named for Dr. Leslie Livingstone, the medical officer on the Canadian Eastern Arctic Patrol.

7. See Alistair Thomas (ed.), *Paddle Quest: Canada's Best Canoe Routes.*

8. Our son Shawn Hodgins, with his spouse, Liz McCarney, had led the first, an adult trip in July 1993. That same year Andrea Hodgins and Michael Craig had led the second, the summer long voyageur co-ed youth trip beginning off the Canol Road near the Yukon-Northwest border, initially on the headwaters of the Tsichu on the Keele Watershed. In 1994, Shawn led another adult trip down the Mountain River with Mark Hodnett as his co-leader, and in July 1995 a Mountain River trip was led by Keva Glenn and Tom Morin.

9. Max Finkelstein, *Canoeing a Continent: On the Trail of Alexander Mackenzie* (Toronto: Natural Heritage Books, 2002). Second printing 2005.
   Max Finkelstein & James Stone, *Paddling the Boreal: Rediscovering A.P. Low* (Toronto: Natural Heritage Books, 2004).

10. All was Mountain River water, but high up in the mountains the headwaters are just tiny streams. At the point where we put into the creek, it was no wider than six feet. and as other mountain streams joined it the water became faster and faster. Someone had named that upper part of the stream Arctic Sky.

11. Jack had left his camouflaged life jacket at a previous lunch spot. Bill and Don had improvised a lifejacket using a thermarest sleeping pad, a belt and some straps. We were not willing to have him paddle through the canyons below without some sort of lifejacket.

12. See Hodgins and Hoyle, *Canoeing North into the Unknown*,

for the South Nahanni River, 140–47; for the Mountain River, 149–51.

13.  Hap Wilson, *Temagami Canoe Routes* (rev. ed.) (Merickville, ON: CRCA, 1988) Map 20, 120-28.

14.  As part of her ORCA work, Sharon Pearson assisting in leading and in writing this log.

15.  See Christopher Norment, *North of Our Lives* (Maine: Down East Books, 1989). Cosmos 94 was a Soviet Radar Ocean Reconnaissance Satellite (RORSAT), which was powered by a nuclear reactor. It went out of control and landed in our Arctic. A piece was found a few kilometres from the Thelon River so all people of the vicinity were evacuated. The Russians did send out a warning about the impending crash. The finding and the cleanup cost about $15 million, and it was only partially paid by the Soviets.

16.  Taken from Carol Hodgins's article, "Thelon Misadventure, 1997," reprinted from the Wilderness Canoeing Association's (WCA) journal, *Nastawgan*, vol. 25, no.3., (Autumn 1998).

**Part Five: A New Millennium with New Adventures, 2000–2007**

1.  For additional background, see Robert Bringhurst and Uli Stelter, *The Black Canoe: Bill Reid and the Spirit of Haida Gwaii* (Vancouver: UBC Press, 1993); and George F. MacDonald, *Chiefs of the Sea and Sky: Haida Heritage Sites of the Queen Charlotte Islands* (Vancouver: Douglas and McIntyre, 1991).

2.  For more information on Hap Wilson and his cabin, see Hap Wilson, *The Cabin: A Search for Personal Sanctuary* (Toronto: Natural Heritage Books, 2005).

3.  Fleming Hill was named after A.L. Fleming, Church of England Bishop of the Arctic, 1933–49. In 1909, he established a Mission in Lake Harbour (now Kimmirut). He was known as the Flying Bishop because of his incredible travels across the Arctic.

4.  See Alistair Thomas, *More of Canada's Best Canoe Routes*, 156–64.

5.   Hap Wilson and Stephanie Ackroyd, *Wilderness Rivers of Manitoba* (Merrickville, ON: CRCA, 1998).

6    For excellent historical accounts on the Killarney-Georgian Bay area see: Margaret E. Derry, *Georgian Bay Jewel: The Killarney Story* (Caledon, ON: Poplar Lane Press, 2007). See also Claire Elizabeth Campbell, *Shaped by the West Wind: Nature and History in Georgian Bay* (Vancouver: UBC Press, 2005).

# Bibliography

Books and Articles on Canoeing and Canoe Tripping by Carol and Bruce Hodgins Including Those Written With Others

Hodgins, Bruce W., "Canoe Irony: Symbol of Wilderness, Harbinger of Destruction," in *Canexus — Canoe in Canadian Culture*, edited by James Raffan and Bert Horwood, Toronto: Betelgeuse, 1988, 45–57.

Hodgins, Bruce W., "1837: To Temagami by Canoe from near Toronto," in *Temagami Times*, January 1979.

Hodgins, Bruce W., "Lady Evelyn River: Where White Falls Roar," in *Paddle Quest: Canada's Best Canoe Routes*, edited by Alister Thomas, Toronto: Stoddart, 2000, 81–86.

Hodgins , Bruce W., "No-Name Trent-Peterborough Canoe Group: A Whimsical History 1966 to 2001," in *More of Canada's Best Canoe Routes*, edited by Alister Thomas, Erin, ON: Boston Mills, 2003, 156–63.

Hodgins, Bruce W., "Refiguring Wilderness: A Personal Odyssey," in *Journal of Canadian Studies*, 33:2 (Summer 1998), 12–26.

Hodgins, Bruce W., "Reflections on a Career of Northern Travelling, Teaching, Writing and Reading," in *Northern Visions: New Perspectives on the North in Canadian History*, edited by Kerry Abel and Ken S. Coates, Peterborough: Broadview Press, 2001, 177–86.

Hodgins, Bruce W., *Wanapitei on Temagami: A Story of Adventures, 1931–2005*. Peterborough: Wanapitei Publishing, 1996.

Hodgins, Bruce W. and Jamie Benidickson, *The Temagami Experience: Recreation, Resources, and Aboriginal Rights in the Northern Ontario Wilderness*. Toronto: University of Toronto Press, 1989.

Hodgins, Bruce W. and Marcus Bruce, "Goin' down the River to James Bay," in *Alternatives* 3:2 (Winter 1974), 13–14.

Hodgins, Bruce W. and Bernadine Dodge (eds.), *Using Wilderness: Essays on the Evolution Of Youth Camping in Ontario,* including the essay by Bruce W. Hodgins and Seana Irvine, "Temagami Youth Camping 1903–1973," 143–56, Peterborough: Frost Centre, Trent University, 1992.

Hodgins, Bruce W., Sandra Gillis, and Kirk Whipper (eds.), *A Log of Canada's Centenary Journey, 1867–1967.* Toronto: Canadian Camping Association, 1971.

Hodgins, Bruce W. and Margaret Hobbs (eds.), *Nastawgan: The Canadian North by Canoe and Snowshoe: A Collection of Historical Essays.* Toronto: Betelgeuse, 1985, including Bruce W. Hodgins's "The Written Word on Canoeing and Canoe Tripping Before 1940," 141–62, and "The Lure of the Temagami-Based Canoe Trip," 189–202.

Hodgins, Bruce W. and Carol Hodgins, "Preserve the Nahanni," in *Wilderness Canoeist* 4:2 (June 1977).

Hodgins, Bruce W. and Gwyneth Hoyle, *Canoeing North Into the Unknown: A Record of River Travel, 1874 to 1974.* Toronto: Natural Heritage Books, 1997.

Hodgins, Bruce W. and Bryan Poirier, "Aboriginal Peoples and the Canoe," in *Hidden in Plain Sight: Contributions of Aboriginal Peoples to Canadian Identity and Culture*, edited by David R. Newhouse, Cora J. Voyageur, and Dan Beavon, Toronto: University of Toronto Press, 2005, 313–27.

Hodgins, Carol. *Wanapitei Canoe Trippers' Cookbook: Wilderness Cooking for Fun and Nutrition.* Cobalt, ON: Highway Book Shop, 1982. Revised edition 2000.

Hodgins, Carol, *Wanapitei Canoe Trippers' Cookbook II: Wilderness Cooking the Environment & You.* Cobalt, ON: Highway Book Shop, 1999.

Hodgins, Carol, "Thelon Misadventure, 1997," in *Nastawgan* 25:3 (Autumn 1998), 1–9.

Jennings, John, Bruce W.Hodgins, and Doreen Small (eds.), *The Canoe in Canadian Cultures,* including Bruce W. Hodgins,

"The Canoe as Chapeau: The Role of the Portage in Canoe Culture," 239–46, Toronto: Natural Heritage Books, 1999.

Marsh, John, Bruce W. Hodgins, Eric R. Hanson. (eds.), *Canada's River Heritage*, including Bruce W. Hodgins "The 1978 Jasper Conference on Heritage Rivers," 25–27, and "Northern River Travel by Canoe, 1874–1974," 48–63, Peterborough: Frost Centre, Trent University, 1996.

McNab, David, Bruce W. Hodgins, Dale Standen, "Black with Canoes: Aboriginal Resistance and the Canoe: Diplomacy, Trade, and Warfare in the Meeting Grounds of Northeastern North America, 1600–1821," in *Technology, Disease and the Colonial Conquests, Sixteenth to Eighteenth Centuries*, edited by George Raudgens, Leiden, Netherlands: Brill Academic Publishers, 2001, 237–292.

## REFERENCE MATERIAL

Many books and articles have been important to us over our fifty years of canoe travel. We would especially like to recommend the two books edited by Alistair Thomas, who first tripped with the two of us on the 1969 Lady Evelyn-Scotia Lake-Onaping Trip. These are mentioned in the section above because Bruce has articles in them, as do Shawn Hodgins ("Snare-Coppermine Rivers") and Glenn Hodgins ("Little Nahanni 1978 and 1998"). Alistair, in his first volume (2000 and 2003) writes a canoeing article on the broadly described "Hodgins Family."

We would like to emphasize three classic works which inspired us. Arthur R.M. Lower's *Unconventional Voyages* (Toronto: Ryerson, 1953) came out while Bruce was studying under him, for his M.A. at Queen's. Back in 1914 Lower had been on a magnificent, full summer canoe trip down the Albany and onto James Bay, along the coast and up the Mattagami back to the train near Cochrane. He was on that trip when World War One broke out, in which he would serve with distinction in the Royal Navy. Being both a Canadian historian and a canoe tripper seemed to fit. Sigurd F. Olson's *The Lonely Land* (New York: Knopf, 1961) describes brilliantly the modern Voyageur group's paddle down the Churchill River and the Sturgeon Weir from Ile-à-la-Crosse to Cumberland House. In 1977, we travelled a little over half of that great historic fur trade route. We carried the book on that trip, and it was a great inspiration. Eric Morse was, of course, with Olson on that trip. Eric Morse was central to the future of these Voyageurs and he would write many tripping books, including *Freshwater Saga* (Toronto: University of Toronto Press, 1987). That historic Churchill trip also included General Elliot Rodger, whose son by the same name married Carol's niece Meredith; the latter two were with us on several of our canoe voyages. With Olson, Morse, and Rodger on that early Churchill trip was Dutch Ambassador Anthony Lovink who had a son also called Tony, who was an early Trent student of Bruce's and one who frequently paddled with us on a couple of day trips.

We have most of Hap Wilson's guide books on canoe routes. Wanapitei heavily uses his frequently revised *Temagami Canoe Routes*. We used it on our 1996 Scarecrow-Snare Creek-Sturgeon Trip. When we were on the Bloodvein River in 2003, his little sketch maps were extremely important to us; the Bloodvein makes up a major section of his and Stephanie Ackroyd's *Wilderness Rivers of Manitoba* (Merrickville: CRCA, 1998).

Our lifelong friend, co-author, former student, and colleague Jamie Benidickson has produced, with his *Paddlers, Water and a Canoe: Reflections on Paddling for Pleasure* (Toronto: University of Toronto Press, 1997), probably the best description of the diverse, historical use of the canoe recreationally and in advertising (where he shows that the canoe has been and can be used to sell almost anything). Brian Back's *The Keewaydin Way: The Story of the World's Oldest Canoe-trip Camp* (Salisbury, VT: Keewaydin Foundation, 2004), is probably the best description ever of the place of northern canoe travel, down through the decades, by a great youth camp. His website, ottertooth.com is a most valuable aid concerning preservation, environmental protection and wilderness political issues and canoe trip descriptions.

We deeply admire Lynn E. Noel's handsome *Voyages: Canada's Heritage Rivers* (St. John's, NL: Breakwater, 1995). Bob Henderson's recent book, *Every Trail has a Story: Heritage Travel in Canada* (Toronto: Natural Heritage Books, 2005) clearly shows and proves the value of travel by canoe and by hiking etc., in vital but safe and enjoyable outdoor education for youths and adults. We agree.

The book by Max Finkelstein and James Stone, *Paddling the Boreal Forest: Rediscovering A.P. Low* (Toronto: Natural Heritage Books, 2004) is a heritage volume, which experientially links the past to the present. The authors travelled through the Cree lands of far Northern Quebec, following the routes that A.P. Low of the Geological Survey of Canada canoed in the early twentieth century.

Then there is John Jennings's *The Canoe: A Living Tradition* (Toronto: Firefly, 2002), which he both edited and was its most important contributor, among many fine contributors. It is undoubtedly the best single book on the nature, diversity and place of the canoe in the Canadian historical experience and in the experience of the United States and several other countries. Long a colleague of Bruce's at Trent, John Jennings has been one of the three or four most important figures in the establishment and early operation of the Canadian Canoe Museum in Peterborough. He and his wife Nicola (Jarvis) Jennings have been friends, canoeing companions and Wanapitei associates ever since the late seventies.

We must mention the importance of the many wonderful canoeing books by James Raffan. His works over the decades are serious, beautiful and well-written, usually with great photographs. We found Raffan's *Summer North of Sixty: By Paddle and Portage Across the Barrenlands* (Toronto: Key Porter, 1990), a book about group dynamics on a long summer trip in the valley of the Thelon River very meaningful. His *Fire in the Bones: Bill Mason and the Canadian Canoeing Tradition* (Toronto: HarperCollins, 1996) is very penetrating and insightful concerning the life of that great Canadian painter, canoe instructor and filmmaker. Raffan's recent editing of Herb Pohl's *The Lure of Faraway Places* (Toronto: Natural Heritage Books, 2007) is a work of great reflection. Pohl, the long-time great solo canoe tripper was drowned off the shore of Lake Superior on August 17, 2006, probably in the same storm that hit us at our campsite off northern Georgian Bay near Killarney. James Raffan's recent publication *Emperor of the North: Sir George Simpson and the Remarkable Story of the Hudson's Bay Company* (Toronto: HarperCollins Publishers Ltd., 2007) is truly magnificent. Only a scholar who is a great canoe tripper, one who knows the classic and many of the not-so-classic canoe routes of Canada could have written such a work, capturing the essence of such a man, with his staggering travel in voyageur canoes or on snowshoes across the country's North and Northwest.

Kevin Callan's prolific works with magnificent photographs are light, humorous and informative with his accessible routes well described. In his *Ontario's Lost Canoe Routes* (Erin, ON: Boston Mills, 2002), he describes "Temagami's Canton Lakes" (128–38). Shawn and Bruce Hodgins were, in a late September in the early nineties, leading a hard canoeing day trip, west from Sharp Rock Inlet of Lake Temagami, with a Trent University (Canadian Studies) field trip through a series of little lakes and ponds joined by overgrown faint portages. Shawn asked what we should call the route. Bruce reflected and then replied: "Well, it is in the obscure geographic township of Canton, so why not call the route the Canton Lakes." A few years later there it was, a chapter in Kevin's book. The canoeing fraternity interacts closely but mysteriously.

Our friend and Bruce's Trent colleague John Wadland has had much to say about the place of the canoe in the Canadian experience. Note especially his "Great Rivers, Small Boats: Landscape and Canadian Historical Culture," in John S. Marsh and Bruce W. Hodgins (eds.), *Changing Parks: The History, Future and Cultural Context of Parks and Heritage Landscapes* (Toronto: Natural Heritage Books Books, 1998).

Craig K. Macdonald, *Historical Map of Temagami (Te-mee-ay-gaming)*, Ontario Geographic Names Board, 1985: This map shows land and watercourses with Aboriginal names, as they existed well before 1900. Macdonald reintroduced the use of the word "Nastawgan," the ways or routes of travel through the waterways and land of the greater Temagami district of northeastern Ontario.

# Index to Lakes, Rivers and Oceans

# Index to People and Places

# About the Authors

Bruce W. Hodgins, PhD, LLD, a recognized authority on canoe travel, is an Emeritus Professor of History, Trent University. He is the author of many books and articles on the North, Aboriginal Peoples, canoeing and comparative federalism. Since 1956 he has been connected with Camp Wanapitei on Lake Temagami, serving as its president since 1972.

Carol Hodgins, born in Charlottetown, Prince Edward Island, a retired physiotherapist, has since 1957 been connected with Camp Wanapitei on Lake Temagami. She has co-led trips with Bruce throughout northern Canada including the Nahanni, Coppermine, Thelon, Mountain and Soper rivers. She has written two Canoe Trippers Cookbooks. She and Bruce live in Peterborough, Ontario.